Your New Dog FOR DUMMIES®

PORTABLE EDITION

by Susan McCullough,
Gina Spadafori, and
M. Christine Zink, DVM, PhD

Wiley Publishing, Inc.

Your New Dog For Dummies®, Portable Edition

Published by
Wiley Publishing, Inc.
111 River St.
Hoboken, NJ 07030-5774
www.wiley.com

For general information on our other products and services, please contact our Customer Care Department within the U.S. at 877-762-2974, outside the U.S. at 317-572-3993, or fax 317-572-4002.

For technical support, please visit www.wiley.com/techsupport.

Wiley also publishes its books in a variety of electronic formats. Some content that appears in print may not be available in electronic books.

ISBN: 978-0-470-76944-7

Manufactured in the United States of America

10 9 8 7 6 5 4 3 2 1

About the Authors

Susan McCullough writes about all things dog for print and online outlets all over the United States. Her dog care books include *Senior Dogs For Dummies* and *Housetraining For Dummies* (Wiley). She is a five-time winner of the Dog Writers Association of America's Maxwell Award for excellence in writing about dogs. She and her family and the family's Golden Retriever live in Vienna, Virginia.

Gina Spadafori is an award-winning columnist who has written about pets and their care for more than 30 years. The first edition of her *Dogs For Dummies* (Wiley) was given the President's Award for the best writing on dogs and the Maxwell Medallion for the best general reference work, both by the Dog Writers Association of America. She and her pets live in Northern California.

Chris Zink is a professor at Johns Hopkins University School of Medicine and has published more than 100 scientific articles. There, she teaches medical and veterinary students and does AIDS research. She also is the author of *Dog Health & Nutrition For Dummies* (Wiley). Chris got her first dog, an Irish Wolfhound, the day she graduated from Ontario Veterinary College with her DVM.

Publisher's Acknowledgments

We're proud of this book; please send us your comments at `http://dummies.custhelp.com`. For other comments, please contact our Customer Care Department within the U.S. at 877-762-2974, outside the U.S. at 317-572-3993, or fax 317-572-4002.

Some of the people who helped bring this book to market include the following:

Acquisitions, Editorial, and Media Development

Project Editor: Victoria M. Adang

Senior Editorial Assistant: David Lutton

Editorial Managers: Jennifer Ehrlich, Michelle Hacker

Editorial Supervisor and Reprint Editor: Carmen Krikorian

Editorial Assistants: Rachelle Amick, Jennette ElNaggar

Cover Photo: © iStock

Cartoon: Rich Tennant (`www.the5thwave.com`)

Composition Services

Project Coordinator: Kristie Rees

Layout and Graphics: Erin Zeltner

Proofreader: Betty Kish

Publishing and Editorial for Consumer Dummies

Diane Graves Steele, Vice President and Publisher, Consumer Dummies

Kristin Ferguson-Wagstaffe, Product Development Director, Consumer Dummies

Ensley Eikenburg, Associate Publisher, Travel

Kelly Regan, Editorial Director, Travel

Publishing for Technology Dummies

Andy Cummings, Vice President and Publisher, Dummies Technology/General User

Composition Services

Debbie Stailey, Director of Composition Services

Contents

Introduction 1

About This Book 1
Conventions Used in This Book 2
Foolish Assumptions 2
Icons Used in This Book 3
Where to Go from Here 3

Chapter 1: So You Have a New Dog! 5

Getting the Goods 5
Shaping Good Behavior 6
Keeping Your Dog Fit with Food and Exercise 8
Paying Attention to Your Pooch's Health 9
If You Haven't Found Your New Dog Yet 11

Chapter 2: Setting Up Your Dog's New Home 13

Providing a Place of His Own 13
Bowls and Waterers 15
Collars and Leashes 16
Encouraging Playtime with Toys 18
Keeping Your Dog Safe in the Great Outdoors 20
Making Sure Your Dog Can Be Identified 23
Protecting Your Dog from Household Hazards 25

Chapter 3: Housetraining Your Canine Companion. . . .29

Planning a Potty Strategy 29
Understanding How Outdoor Training Works 32
Training Your Pooch to Go Potty Outdoors 33
Dealing with Oopsies 38

Chapter 4: Communicating and Teaching Basic Manners 41

DogSpeak 101: Figuring Out How to Communicate with Your Pet 41
Training the Polite Pooch 46

Chapter 5: Day-to-Day Care for Your Dog 49

Fulfilling Basic Nutritional Needs 49
Choosing Food for Fido 51
Treating Your Dog 53
Understanding the Benefits of Exercise 54
Mixing Up Your Dog's Exercise Routine 55
Getting the Gear for Grooming 58
Keeping Up Appearances 61

Chapter 6: Keeping Your Dog Healthy 67

Vaccinating Your Dog 67
Neutering Your Dog 68
Getting Rid of Fleas, Ticks, and Worms 69
Assembling a Canine First-Aid Kit 73
Giving First-Aid Treatment 77

Chapter 7: Ten Tips for Traveling with Your Dog 85

Travel Manners Are a Must 85
Pack a Doggie Suitcase 86
Bring Emergency Papers 87
Make Car Rides Safer 87
Help Your Dog Keep Her Cool 87
Travel by Air 88
Find Dog-Friendly Quarters 89
Choose a Doggie Resort 89
Try Ruffing It! 90
If Your Dog Can't Go with You 90

Introduction

Welcome to *Your New Dog For Dummies,* the canine reference for those who want all the basics covered in one easy-to-use book. If you're looking for information about dog gear, dog grooming, dog health, and dog training, you've found it.

This book can help you get to know your new dog, while maintaining your role as Top Dog in your household. You discover how to tend to your dog's day-to-day needs, teach her how to be a well-behaved companion, and provide for her health and nutritional needs.

About This Book

Nobody adopts a dog guessing that they'll be dropping him off at the shelter later. Just thinking about doing so is heartbreaking. You get a dog because you want a loving, well-mannered companion. A playmate for the children. A crime deterrent, perhaps.

The most important factors in determining whether you end up with your dream dog or an ill-mannered and possibly dangerous beast are how well you educate yourself about your dog's needs and how well you educate your dog thereafter.

We've taken what you need to know about parenting a pooch and put it in this book. Of course, no book can cover every detail about being a doggie daddy or mommy, but we're sure you'll form a successful relationship by using the information in the following pages.

Conventions Used in This Book

To help you find your way through this book — as in all *For Dummies* books — we've used the following conventions:

- *Italics* highlight new words and terms.
- **Boldfaced** text indicates the actions in numbered steps and keywords in bulleted lists.
- `Monofont` indicates a Web address.

Then there's the matter of gender. Many writers like to refer to canine companions in gender-neutral terms such as *it* unless discussing a specific dog, such as Daisy or Max. But we don't agree with them. Any dog, even if spayed or neutered, has a clear gender. More important, every dog is a living being who deserves the dignity of being referred to as such. For that reason, we use the word *who,* not *that,* along with *he, she, him, her, his,* and *hers* to refer to canine companions. We tend to alternate the genders of the example dogs in a chapter, so any of those pronouns (or a name such as Fido or Lassie) applies to dogs of either gender unless we indicate otherwise.

Foolish Assumptions

We've written this book assuming that one of the following scenarios applies to you:

- You're seriously thinking about adopting a dog for the first time.
- You've adopted a dog, but you're not sure what specific gear your dog needs.
- You have some experience with dogs, but you want a refresher course in basic care and training.
- You're overwhelmed with the array of toys and supplies and food choices and want some guidance on which items are right for your dog.

If you fit into any of the preceding categories, this book is for you.

Icons Used in This Book

To make this book simpler to use, we've included some icons to help you find and fathom key ideas and information.

This icon reminds you of information so important that you should read it more than once, just to make sure it stays with you.

This icon flags things that are especially useful for making living with your dog easier or making your dog happier and healthier.

This icon marks some of the most common mistakes dog owners make, along with tips for avoiding them.

Where to Go from Here

If you're brand-new to dog ownership, we suggest you start with Chapter 1 and continue with the subsequent chapters to get the lowdown on what it's like to live with and love a dog.

If you've owned a dog before but it's been a while, check out the table of contents to see what interests you. Maybe you need help teaching your new pooch the finer points of going to the bathroom; flip to Chapter 3. If you want to teach your dog some basic commands like "Sit" or "Stay," Chapter 4 can help.

One thing we're sure of: With the information that follows in this book, you're well on your way to becoming a dog expert — and better still, a satisfied dog owner.

The 5th Wave By Rich Tennant

"That's actually the dog's wee-wee pad, Doug. I don't want to confuse him, so you should either do something on it or step off."

Chapter 1

So You Have a New Dog!

In This Chapter

- Picking up the basic supplies
- Remembering that manners matter
- Providing food and exercise
- Minding your dog's health
- Looking for a dog in all the right places

"Acquiring a dog may be the only opportunity a human ever has to choose a relative," writes author Mordecai Siegal, and that may explain part of the excitement that you and your family experience when you bring home a new dog of any description, young or old. And as far as the pooch goes, she wants to be part of a family, a pack.

In return for your new dog's love and companionship, she needs you to take care of her basic needs. Those include shelter, food and water, and exercise, but throwing in some tempting treats and terrific toys doesn't hurt either. Most important, your dog wants your affection and approval, so spending time with your dog is also a must. In this chapter, we introduce you to the basics of caring for your new furry friend.

Getting the Goods

The best part of getting a dog is getting *your* dog. The second best part may be getting all the gear your new dog needs. We recommend making your first run to the pet supply store without your canine companion. If you're getting an adult dog, you may not know how he'll behave around strangers or in an unfamiliar environment. If you're getting a puppy, you shouldn't let your puppy venture into places where other dogs have been until he's received all of his vaccinations (see Chapter 6 for more on vaccinations).

Here's your shopping list:

- Brush and comb
- Chew toys
- Dishwasher-safe, nonchewable bowls: one for water, one for food
- Pet stain cleaner
- Flat or rolled collar, buckle or snap-together — not a slip (choke) collar — with an ID tag

  Don't worry if you haven't named your dog yet. Let his first ID tag just say REWARD instead of a name. The important thing is to get one on him, right away.

- High-quality food, as recommended by the breeder, shelter, or veterinarian
- Lightweight leash, 6-feet long
- Nail trimmer and Kwik Stop powder
- Pooper scooper and plastic bags
- Properly sized crate
- Dog shampoo

The lowdown on all of these items, such as the proper kind of brush or comb, and the proper type and size of crate, is in Chapters 2 and 5.

Shaping Good Behavior

Your dog starts learning the moment he's born. If you've adopted a puppy, by the time he's 7 to 10 weeks of age, he's as absorbent as a bath towel, taking in the sights and sounds of his world and trying to figure out his place in it. The position he decides he has may be quite different from the one you want him to have, which is why you need to be involved in the process as he learns to live with his new, human family.

It's not that complicated, really, to train puppies or older dogs. Your pooch wants to be part of your family, and he craves loving leadership. Just keep a few things in mind as you enjoy your new friend:

- Socialize your dog and bond with him.
- If you have a puppy, never let him do anything you wouldn't want a grown dog to do.
- Teach your dog using positive methods — make training fun!
- Realize your dog will make mistakes, and don't get angry when he does.
- Remember always that preventing bad habits is easier than fixing them later.

If you have a bad attitude toward training, your dog will too. If you think training is a joyless chore, he'll hate it. If you walk around jerking on his collar and swearing, he'll wonder what he's done to deserve your anger, and he'll be too busy worrying about that to learn anything.

Expect success from your dog and be willing to work for it. Praise him not only for succeeding, but for trying. Learning is hard for him, and stressful. Think of your dog as a person who has just moved to your house from a country where the language and customs are different — a trans-species exchange student. He was born, after all, a dog, and you're asking him to live as a member of a human family. You're asking him to learn the language and follow the rules.

The fact that this feat is ever accomplished at all is nothing less than a miracle. So celebrate it. With him.

Consider dog training not as a mechanical thing — if you do X, your dog does Y — but rather as something organic — alive, interconnected, and ever-changing. A well-mannered dog becomes that way from the inside out. "Sit" and "Stay" are the least of it, really, and are only the visible manifestations of what that dog is on the inside: a confident, comfortable, and secure member of a loving, human pack. A dog who is, quite simply, a joy to live with. (For more details about training your pooch, see Chapter 4.)

If you start a training session fine and feel yourself getting frustrated and angry, don't push things. End on a positive note. Ask your dog for something you know he knows well and, when he does it, praise him. Then call it a day. If you can't manage even that, just stop before you both get even more frustrated.

Keeping Your Dog Fit with Food and Exercise

If you're like most people, when you look at the shelves of dog food in the store, you're bewildered by the choices available to you. There are puppy foods and senior foods; foods for large dogs and foods for small dogs; diet foods for pudgy pooches; foods that claim to be all-natural; foods that make promises about how they'll improve your dog's coat; foods that make their own gravy; and foods shaped like little bones.

How can you possibly pick the best food for your furry friend — a food that will give him all the nutrients he needs and help him to live a long and healthy life? Worry not. In Chapter 5, we describe the meat and potatoes of feeding your dog. The information will help you make better choices when you're buying dog food.

And of course, what goes in must come out. Some of your pup's dog food comes out in the form of pee and poop; we cover housetraining basics in Chapter 3.

The food that stays in your dog fuels your dog's body. What to do with all of that doggie energy? Exercise, of course!

Does the word *exercise* evoke images in your mind of runners with sweaty shirts, glazed eyes, and sore feet? Don't worry; you can exercise your dog without sweating beside your panting pup over miles of hot pavement. Many more interesting and effective ways of providing your dog with the exercise she needs are at your disposal. With a little imagination, you can invent a variety of exercises and games that will build your dog's strength and endurance and that you'll both enjoy (check out Chapter 5 to get your creative juices flowing). Exercise takes a little time, but the payoff is enormous in terms of your dog's health and vitality, her confidence and behavior, and your relationship with her. Besides, who among us can't use a few moments of stress-free playtime during the day?

Paying Attention to Your Pooch's Health

The first step in taking care of your dog is knowing what he should look like when he is healthy. If you know what a healthy dog looks like, you'll be better able to know when your dog is sick and to get him the help he needs.

Determining whether a dog is healthy is difficult because dogs can't talk to us in our language and tell us how they are feeling. So being good observers — using all of our senses to gather information about our dogs' health — is especially important. Our eyes show us the glistening coat and wagging tail of a healthy dog. Our hands tell us that the healthy dog's skin is smooth and supple. Our ears hear the deep, regular breathing of a healthy dog as he sleeps. Even our noses get involved as they smell the fresh breath of a dog with healthy teeth and gums. The following list gives you some clues about what to look for in assessing your dog's health.

- **Appetite:** A hungry dog is usually a healthy dog. Most dogs consume their meals in five minutes or less. One of the first signs of illness is a decreased interest in food.
- **Attitude:** A healthy dog exudes a love of life. His head is up, his eyes are bright, and his tail wags with the expectation of fun. Your dog should be energetic, inquisitive, and interested in new surroundings. If you notice a shift in your dog's attitude that continues for more than two days, this may be a sign of other problems.
- **Coat:** The coat is a good indicator of a dog's overall health. A healthy dog should have a shiny, springy coat. In addition, the skin under all that hair should be soft and supple. When you pinch your dog's skin, it should spring back to its original position. If the hair seems dull, dry, and broken, or if an area of hair was shaved but isn't growing back normally, have your dog examined by a veterinarian, especially if he is exhibiting other signs of illness.
- **Ears:** The ears of a healthy dog should be clean inside, with a shiny gleam to the skin that is caused by the secretion of a protective waxy substance. A healthy dog's

ears should not have excessive wax, however, and the ears should never have a foul odor. If your dog's ears have a black or dark brown discharge that recurs after cleaning, they could be infected.

- **Eyes:** A healthy dog has bright, clear, glistening eyes. The *cornea* (the outermost surface of the eye) should be transparent, and you should be able to clearly see the pupil and the tiny folds of the *iris* (the brown or blue ring that gives the eye its color).
- **Gums and teeth:** A healthy dog should have shiny gums that are tightly adherent to the teeth. Light-colored dogs tend to have pink gums, whereas dark-colored dogs and dogs that are bred to have blue tongues tend to have gums that are splotched with brown and black. The teeth should be white and shiny, without any buildup of brown or yellow material adjacent to the gum line.
- **Nose:** The nose is a good barometer of your dog's overall health. It should be cold and wet. But your dog's nose may become a little dry when he is sleeping, so don't panic if your snoozing canine doesn't have a slick schnoz.
- **Pulse:** The resting heart of a healthy dog will beat anywhere from 40 beats a minute (in large breeds) to 120 beats a minute (in Toy breeds). Your dog's heart rate increases when he has a fever or when he is feeling pain, so if you think your dog may be feeling ill, check his pulse as one indicator of a potential problem.
- **Stools:** The stools of a healthy dog are formed and easy to scoop. They can be any color from light to dark brown. Black stools, however, are not normal and may be a sign of gastrointestinal bleeding. An occasional loose stool is normal in dogs, but continued loose stools or even one episode of very watery diarrhea are reason to schedule a veterinary visit.
- **Weight:** A healthy dog has a slight waist and an abdomen that is tucked up higher than the level of his chest. A healthy dog should be able to trot effortlessly without the skin and *subcutaneous fat* (the fat that is located under the skin) rolling from side to side.

Chapter 6 contains more information about canine health and first aid. We recommend that you read it now so you know what to do when your dog gets sick or has an emergency.

If You Haven't Found Your New Dog Yet

You can find puppies and dogs through many sources — examples include breeders, shelters, and pet stores. Although locating the perfect pet is at times trying and difficult, someone, somewhere, has a wonderful pet for you. As an informed consumer you want to maximize the chances of coming up with a healthy and temperamentally sound dog. In the following sections, we take a look at three sources for finding the dog of your dreams.

Shelters: A good choice and a good deed

Today's shelter pets are more adoptable than ever before, thanks to programs that temperament test and perform basic health services before animals are made available to the public. The best shelters have well-trained, caring staffs and a healthy core of volunteers to keep dogs socialized and counsel potential adopters as to the animal that will provide the best match with their circumstances.

Some shelters are run by municipal animal-control facilities, and some are run by nonprofit humane organizations. Some of the latter have widely different policies that determine the kind of dogs they have available for adoption.

Making a decision about a shelter dog is often difficult. You want to take them all, and the realization that some of these dogs aren't going to find a new home softens even the hardest heart. But you aren't doing anyone any favors if you let your heart make your decision. If you pass over a dog who suits you better because of one you felt sorrier for, the dog you should have taken — the one that would have worked — may not make it. And you may end up miserable with your choice to the point where you take him back and don't try again.

Take a friend to keep you from making a foolish decision. And take your time. Go back a few times if you have to.

Be aware of some potential problems with going to a shelter. Shelter puppies are at risk for contracting highly contagious diseases such as parvovirus and kennel cough.

In addition, most shelters spay or neuter your dog before you take her or him home, or they require it done as a condition of adoption. Some also screen you almost as thoroughly as an adoption agency might, to make sure you're "qualified" to have a dog — and turn you down if they decide you're not! These are understandable policies for organizations on the front lines of fighting pet overpopulation.

Finding a good breeder

A reputable breeder can be very hard to find and may not have a puppy available when you want one. Those facts alone send many puppy buyers to other sources. But consider the advantages of adding your name to a waiting list and adopting through a reputable breeder.

The serious breeder can tell you more than you possibly imagined about the breed. Their commitment to the puppy you buy doesn't end when the sale is final. You get a healthy, well-socialized puppy, as well as technical support that would be the envy of any software company. A serious breeder is just too good to pass up.

Private parties

Every year, countless people advertise dogs as "free to a good home" in newspapers and on office bulletin boards, or for sale at what may seem to be a good price. These people aren't trying to move the merchandise, but just have a dog or two who needs a new home.

Some of the people who put up these ads are trying to find homes for a stray, or help out a friend or neighbor in a pinch who has to place a dog, or are giving a dog they can no longer care for another shot at a good life. Some good dogs have turned up this way, but remember to let your head, not your heart, be your guide. Ask your questions, and if you don't get the answers you want, don't consider adopting the dog, no matter how sad the story.

Chapter 2

Setting Up Your Dog's New Home

In This Chapter

- Choosing basic dog gear
- Picking a proper fence
- Providing a set of dog tags
- Keeping your dog safe from household hazards

A dog can get by without much in the way of material belongings and a great many of them do. A collar. A leash. A container for water, and one for food. A warm, dry place to sleep. Something to play with or chew on. Add love, training, and attention to the list and, in truth, a dog doesn't need much more.

But you'll also want to keep your dog safe. That means providing protection and shelter when she's outdoors, making sure she has the proper identification in case you and she get separated, and keeping her from chowing down on seemingly tasty but harmful foods and chemicals. This chapter contains what you need to know to create a comfy home for your canine companion.

Providing a Place of His Own

Dogs love to have a safe, protected place of their own. They will sleep under a low table or in a quiet corner of the room. Or you can provide your dog with a crate to fulfill his need for seclusion and security. You can also purchase a doggie bed that offers your pup many of the creature comforts he could want.

Crates

Much of what you can buy for your dog probably isn't necessary for his health and well-being, but if you're making a list of things to buy, a crate should be at the top of it. *Crates* are plastic or metal cages with a door at one end. You can find them in pet-supply stores or catalogs. A crate is your dog's home within your home — a safe place he can go to escape the crowd. It's also a place you can put him when he needs a timeout. One of the greatest benefits of a crate is that it makes housetraining a breeze. See Chapter 3 for more details.

When you first bring your new dog home, put some treats in the crate to encourage your hesitant hound to step inside. If you give him his dinner in the crate, he will love being there even more. When he's used to the crate, close the door for gradually longer periods of time. Never put your dog in his crate for punishment. When your dog is comfortable in his doggie den, you can confine him there when you're out of the house or otherwise unable to supervise him. When you return, immediately take your dog outside and praise him when he eliminates, making it clear to him that urinating outside is the only acceptable option.

Do not confine your dog in a crate if he shows signs of intense anxiety when left alone. Locking him in a crate at this time can cause him to panic and injure himself. It also may make his separation anxiety worse.

What size crate should you get? If your dog is an adult, take him to the store and, using an ample supply of treats, try several crates on for size. Get a crate that allows your dog to lie flat on his side with his legs outstretched and to stand up without having to duck his head. If you're getting a crate for a young pup, get one that will be suitable for him when he is full-grown. If you're debating between two sizes, get the larger one.

While your pup is still growing, you can put a plastic divider inside the dog crate to make it temporarily smaller. Otherwise, he may learn to pee on one end and sleep on the other.

Beds

Indoor dogs need a place to sleep, too. Unless your dog has impeccable manners and respects your authority, he shouldn't be on your bed — it gives him the wrong idea concerning who's the Top Dog in your family. Don't feel sorry for him, though: More beautiful and comfortable beds are available today than ever before, to fit every dog, every budget, and every decor.

The best dog beds are made of foam, synthetic batting, or cedar chips enclosed in a washable cover. Many dogs like to lie with their heads slightly elevated. If your pooch has this propensity, you can get him a bed shaped like a donut, with a hollowed out center and a raised edge. Many dog beds and cots are available at pet supply stores. Before you get a dog bed, however, ask if you can bring your dog into the store to test the bed out.

If you plan to invest in a dog bed, make sure it is big enough for your dog to toss, turn, and lie in any position he wants. Although they are quaint, most wicker beds are not suitable for dogs because their hard, raised sides and rounded shape force a dog to sleep in a curled position.

Bowls and Waterers

In dog dishes, too, you have a lot of options, from using an old pot to buying a hand-thrown ceramic bowl with your dog's name painted on it. Dishes designed to store up to a couple of days' worth of food or water are available.

Look for sturdy dishes of molded, high-impact plastic or stainless steel that resist chewing or scratching and can be sterilized in the dishwasher. These dishes — stainless steel especially — retain their good looks, handle any abuse a dog can dish out, and last forever. Dishes that damage easily are hard to keep clean and invite the buildup of food and bacteria in the dents and scratches. Some dogs also have a sensitivity to flimsy plastic bowls.

For dogs with long, silky ears — like Cocker Spaniels — look for bowls with a narrow opening and high, sloped sides to keep that fur out of the muck. If your dog is a ravenous eater, a bowl with a nonskid base will help keep the dish from ending up in the next county.

While your dog's food dishes should be picked up, washed, and put away after meals, water dishes need to be kept full and available at all times. Here, too, stainless steel is your best choice. Dishes with reservoirs are fine, but they can be hard to keep clean. And, unless your dog needs a lot of water, these products get mucky before the water needs to be refilled.

Collars and Leashes

Collars, harnesses, halters, and leashes perform a very vital function: They help you to train your dog and allow you to keep him out of trouble in public. Collars also protect your dog when you can't, by carrying identification that will get him home should he ever slip away from you.

When ordering a collar — buckled or quick-snap — for regular wear, measure a couple of inches down the neck from your dog's head, and then add 2 inches. For tiny dogs, add 1 inch. When trying on collars, you should be able to fit two fingers snugly between collar and neck; one finger on a small dog. The goal is to have a collar snug enough so your dog can't back up and out of the collar, but loose enough for comfort.

The everyday collar

A collar is an essential purchase for your dog, but if he's wearing the wrong collar at the wrong time, your dog could end up hurt or even dead, which is why learning a little before you go shopping is important.

Your pet's everyday collar, the one you put her tags on, should be a buckled collar, either flat or rolled, made of nylon web or leather. Either a flat collar or a rolled collar will work fine on dogs with short or medium fur, but rolled collars are preferable on dogs with thick, long fur at the neck, such as Collies.

Nylon web collars come in an incredible variety of colors and patterns. Some dogs may find a nylon collar irritating and do better with leather. As long as the collar is well made, both nylon and leather will last for years. In recent years, quick-snap closures have become popular, especially on flat nylon web collars. And it's easy to see why: Press in at the edges and the collar's off easily for baths and changing tags. Press the tips together and snap, it's on again.

Leashes

Leashes usually are made of leather or nylon or cotton webbing. Many people prefer leather leashes because they are soft on the hands and easy to grip. Leather leashes do stretch over time, however, and they break more easily than nylon or cotton ones do. Plus, when they're wet, the leather dye can stain your dog's fur and your hands or clothes. Nylon webbing is the strongest and most durable material for leashes. It comes in many different colors and widths. Nylon leashes, however, are sometimes difficult to hold onto when a strong dog is pulling. Cotton leashes are easier to grip, but they're less durable than nylon.

Avoid leashes made of chain. Although they're strong, they can cause injuries if they inadvertently get wrapped around an arm or a leg. In addition, they usually have plastic or nylon handles that are easily separated from the chain, putting the dog at risk of escaping.

As a general rule, the shorter the leash, the greater your control; the longer the leash, the greater your dog's freedom. Many people find a 6-foot leash a good compromise when taking a walk. It lets your dog wander in a 12-foot diameter around you, but you still can reel him in quickly when necessary. With a little experience, you can learn to hold the leash so your dog won't get his legs tangled in it, and your dog will learn to untangle himself if he does.

If you're taking your dog out to exercise in a park or another recreation area that requires her to be kept on leash, consider using a retractable leash. Retractable leashes are very popular because they give your dog a great deal of freedom while still providing you with some control. Retractable leashes have a short length of nylon webbing that snaps to your dog's collar. The nylon webbing is attached to a spring-loaded cord that comes out of and retracts into a plastic handle. Pushing a button on the handle causes the cord to be locked in position. So your dog can run out to a distance of 15 feet or more and return to you without getting tangled in the leash. You can control the distance your dog strays by using the locking mechanism.

Never let go of the handle of a retractable leash when it is attached to a dog. The handle will spring toward the snap and can badly injure a human or dog in its way. Projectile retractable leashes have seriously injured or knocked unconscious dogs and humans.

Be sure to obey your local leash laws. In more and more areas of the country, dogs are not allowed at all. A major reason for this is the inconsiderate behavior *not* of dogs, but of their people, who let their dogs roam, bothering people and wildlife, and leaving canine messes behind. Be sure you don't contribute to that problem.

Encouraging Playtime with Toys

Playtime is essential for a dog's mental and physical health. Young puppies play as soon as they can walk, which helps them grow and develop correctly and teaches them about their environment. It also helps them learn the social skills they need to get along with other dogs and with humans. Most adult dogs like to play, too. Play helps relieve stress and keeps adult dogs physically fit. By selecting your dog's toys wisely and by participating in games with your dog, you can make his play more interesting, you can strengthen your bond with your dog, and you can make sure your dog plays safely.

Chewies

The best way to keep your home furnishings intact is to provide a variety of chew toys for your dog. Test your dog with a number of toys to see how aggressive a chewer he is. Frequently, Sporting dogs are gentle chewers because they have been bred to have soft mouths so that they don't destroy the birds they retrieve. Chew toys last a lot longer for these dogs than for more assertive chewers. Tough, latex squeaky toys, stuffed toys with squeakers, and rope toys all are great for passionate chewers.

Some of the toughest chew toys on the market are made by Nylabone, in a variety of sizes, shapes, and colors. The king of chew toys is the Kong, a hard rubber toy that looks a little like the Michelin Tire man. Not only are Kongs almost impossible to destroy, they bounce in a sprightly manner, in unpredictable directions.

Rawhide bones, sterilized real *long bones* (the bones of the leg) purchased from pet supply stores or catalogs, and *dental bones* (bumpy, hard plastic bones designed to clean the chewer's teeth) all are excellent outlets for the canine chewer. The chewing motion helps remove plaque and *calculus* (hard mineral build-up) from dogs' teeth, and it also massages the gums.

Dogs should be supervised whenever they chew a new toy for the first time to be sure they don't break off and swallow pieces of it.

Supervise your dog when he is chewing a rawhide bone because he may soften a large piece, try to swallow it, and choke. If your dog has had a fractured tooth, don't let him chew real bones or other hard objects.

Fetchies

Fetch is an outstanding way to exercise your dog while reminding him of your role as pack leader. Many people use flying discs for this and, while it's great fun, you should be aware that some dogs have been injured while leaping after flying discs, to the point of needing surgery on their knees and backs.

Tennis balls are another common toy with built-in risks. Never let your dog chew on a tennis ball or play with one unattended. Some dogs have died after a tennis ball, compressed by powerful jaws, popped into the throat and cut off the air supply.

Does that mean you should avoid playing with flying discs or tennis balls? No, but use some common sense. With flying discs, avoid the acrobatics that wow spectators at half-time shows but have your dog leaping, twisting, and landing hard. Work on low throws in front of your dog, to encourage him to run, but not to jump. Try floppy discs made of fabric, not plastic. Tennis balls are fine for fetch, but put them away when the game's over.

Tug toys

Many dogs love to play tug-of-war, whether it's with a leash, a stick, or a toy designed for tugging. Rope toys, balls with a rope or bungie cord attached, and rubber toys shaped in a figure eight are all designed to help you satisfy your dog's desire to tug.

Some people mistakenly think they should not let a dog play tug because it may make the dog more dominant and aggressive. But I believe that playing tug is perfectly okay as long as you have control of the game. Teach your dog that he must obey you when you tell him to let go. And make sure you maintain control by asking your dog to stop every now and then.

Toys that educate and occupy

You don't need to feel guilty when you leave for work, knowing that your dog will be alone all day. Instead, give him a toy that will keep him occupied for several hours. A beef leg bone stuffed with peanut butter will keep your dog busy sticking his tongue down the marrow hole, trying to get every last morsel. You also can stuff a rubber Kong toy (which is shaped like a beehive and has an open, stuffable center) with some cookies, seal it with cream cheese or peanut butter, and let him dig out the treasures.

A *Buster Cube* is a 6-inch square (for large dogs) or 3-inch square (for small dogs) cube with a hole in one end into which you can deposit dog food or other small morsels. To release the treats, your dog must move the cube with his nose or paw, tilting the cube just so. The Buster Cube is a great toy to occupy dogs and to hone their problem-solving abilities. This toy can keep a dog occupied for hours, hunting for just the right way to expel the food.

Keeping Your Dog Safe in the Great Outdoors

Although you may never intend for your dog to be running loose, dogs have a way of sneaking out when you're not looking. So in the following sections, we give you some suggestions for keeping your dog confined.

Choosing a traditional fence

Whether your dog sleeps in the lap of luxury or roughs it, he should not be allowed to run free. Loose dogs are likely to be hit by cars, and they frequently chase wild animals. If their chase instinct gets the better of them and they run after sheep or other farm animals, they could be shot. If they haven't been spayed or castrated, they will likely contribute to the problem of dog overpopulation. And small stray dogs frequently are carried off by birds such as eagles or vultures. Because of these hazards, dogs who are allowed to roam free do not live as long and do not remain as healthy as their confined counterparts.

A walk around a postage stamp-size backyard is not enough exercise for a medium or large dog. Daily exercise helps keep your dog trim, healthy, and happy, and he will live longer, too (see Chapter 5 for more information on exercising your dog).

A fence is the best choice to keep your pooch on your property for a number of reasons. A fence provides a visible barrier that not only keeps your dog in, but it also keeps other dogs out — a definite advantage in city neighborhoods where dogs often roam loose. A split-rail fence lined by woven wire makes an attractive, effective, and relatively inexpensive fence. Some people prefer solid fences such as *stockade fences* which provide more privacy for a dog who feels the need to guard his property from every passerby. This advantage also can be a disadvantage, however. Dogs kept behind solid fences may not be as acclimatized to the sights and sounds of the neighborhood and may be more fearful when they're not on their home turf.

A 4-foot fence adequately confines most dogs. A few dogs can jump a 4-foot fence and require a 6-foot fence. Occasionally, dogs learn how to climb fences. These canine escape artists require smooth-sided, 6-foot stockade fences or kennels with enclosed roofs.

Don't tie your dog up by a chain or rope. Dogs who are tied often become frustrated as they bark and lunge at passing dogs, people, and wild animals. Typically, chained or tied dogs are more aggressive to strangers and other dogs, even when they are loose.

Going high-tech with an electronic fence

Unfortunately, many suburban developments prohibit the fencing of property, necessitating the use of other confinement methods. One of the most popular is the *electronic fence,* which uses an electrical circuit buried a few inches underground at the perimeter of the property. The dog wears a battery-operated collar that, when in close proximity to the buried wire, closes an electrical circuit and provides a shock to the dog's neck. The dog initially is trained to recognize the boundary by the presence of small, flagged stakes. After the dog has learned his boundaries, you can remove the flags.

Electronic fences are subject to a number of problems. First, it doesn't prevent other dogs from entering your yard, so neighborhood dogs can come over and harass your canine companion. In addition, your dog may play with a visiting dog in your yard or chase a squirrel and accidentally cross the fence. If this happens, the shock then prevents your dog from re-entering your yard. Finally, as with all electronic gadgets, these fences are subject to failure. They may fail because the power has been shut off, because the battery in the dog's collar has not been sufficiently charged, or because the dog was let outside without his collar on (just this once).

Don't include your front yard in the area surrounded by an electronic fence. Your dog will be more likely to become a nuisance by barking at strangers who walk by. Plus, some dogs develop territorial aggression because of the constant stimulation of cars and children walking along the front of their property. It's best to confine your dog to your backyard.

If you use an electronic fence, don't leave the collar on your dog when he's indoors. In addition, check the area under his collar every day. The collar must be worn tight so the metal prongs contact your dog's skin. If the collar is too tight or the skin gets wet, however, a bacterial infection can develop.

Don't assume your dog is perfectly safe just because you've installed an electronic fence. Check on your dog every few minutes when he's outdoors. Animal-control officers say that many dogs killed on the road are wearing electronic collars.

Doghouses: Protection from the elements

If your dog spends much time outside — while you're at work, perhaps — he needs shelter from heat and cold. One of the easiest ways to provide this is a doghouse. Your choices here: wood or high-impact plastic.

No matter the material you choose, a doghouse should fit your pet snugly — he should be able to stand up and turn around, but not much more. Providing your dog with a house that's too large makes staying warm inside of it difficult for him. It should have an entrance that's off-center so the dog can curl up in one end for warmth. A removable roof is helpful for easy cleaning, and the doorway should have a flap over it to keep drafts out.

Several manufacturers offer doghouses of molded, high-impact plastic that are in some ways superior to traditional wooden ones. They clean easily, do not retain smells and offer no place for fleas to breed.

Where you place the doghouse has a lot to do with how comfortable your dog is when in it. In winter, it should be in a spot that's protected from the wind. And in summer, it should be in the shade.

Making Sure Your Dog Can Be Identified

One of the more important things you can do as a dog owner is give your dog ample identification so if he escapes, others will be able to identify him and return him to you right away. You can accomplish this in several ways, all outlined in the following sections.

Tags

Military servicemen call their ID tags *dog tags* for a reason. Both types of dog tags are essential to identify the wearer in case he is lost or injured. The vast majority of dogs in animal shelters were not wearing identification tags when they were found, making it much more difficult for the dogs to be reunited with their owners.

Make sure your dog is always wearing an ID tag with your name, address, and telephone number on it. You also may want to include the dog's name on the tag and other pertinent information, such as the name and telephone number of your veterinarian.

In the U.S. and Canada, the law requires all dogs to be vaccinated for rabies. You can save yourself, your dog, and others a great deal of trouble and worry if you make sure that your dog wears his rabies tag at all times. If your dog is lost and ends up biting a stranger, the veterinarian or animal control officer will know that your dog has been vaccinated against rabies. They also may be able to contact you through the number on the tag.

Make sure your dog wears his collar and tags all the time. It can save his life. And you never know when your dog will dash out the door after a squirrel in the yard or when a well-intentioned appliance repairperson will let your dog out. If your dog wears a collar and ID tags at all times, the person who finds him will be able to get in touch with you no matter what.

Tattoos

Many dog owners use tattoos to permanently identify their dogs. Tattoos can be placed on the skin inside the ear, on the lower stomach where the hair is thinner, or on the inside of the thigh. Puppies as young as 7 weeks can be tattooed. A tattoo usually costs between $10 and $20.

Get an experienced canine tattoo artist to do the job. Tattooing is a permanent procedure, and you want the tattoo to remain clear throughout your dog's life. Ask your veterinarian for a referral.

Before getting your dog tattooed, check with various registries that record tattoo numbers and help reunite lost, tattooed dogs with their owners. Different registries may suggest that you include specific information on the tattoo. The National Dog Registry, for example, one of the foremost registries for dog tattoos, suggests that you tattoo your dog with your Social Security number, because you will have this number your entire life. If you decide to use your Social Security number, add one or more additional digits that are unique to each of your dogs; that way, each of your dogs is identified individually. You also can tattoo your purebred dog with his American Kennel Club (AKC) registration number or use another unique registration number. After your dog has been tattooed, be sure to register him with your chosen registry. You don't need to register your dog with more than one. The following organizations offer registration of tattooed dogs:

- National Dog Registry (phone: 800-637-3647; Web site: `www.nationaldogregistry.com`)
- Tattoo-a-Pet (phone: 800-828-8667; Web site: `www.tattoo-a-pet.com`)

Always include the telephone number of your dog's tattoo registry on his ID tag.

Microchips

Thanks to digital technology, your dog can be identified by a tiny microchip the size of a grain of rice. Your veterinarian can insert a microchip with a unique identification number under the skin at the back of your dog's neck, where it will remain for the rest of his life.

As with tattoos, register your dog's microchip number with an organization that reunites lost dogs with their owners. The best and most commonly used organization is the AKC Companion Animal Recovery (phone: 800-252-7894; Web site: `www.akc.org`).

If your dog is lost, a veterinarian or animal shelter worker can use an electronic scanner to read the ID numbers on the microchip. They then can contact the registry and get your name, address, and telephone number.

Always include the telephone number of your dog's microchip registry on his ID tag.

Protecting Your Dog from Household Hazards

Dogs are great explorers, ever curious to see what new scents and tastes they can find in the environment. Like toddlers, they put everything in their mouths to see what tastes good, what has an interesting texture, and what may be used to practice their chewing techniques. As a result, dogs frequently are exposed to toxic or hazardous items. People with children are careful to place dangerous items out of the reach of children, but dogs frequently go places where children don't (like the garage) — and some things that aren't toxic for children are quite dangerous for dogs (like chocolate). Dog-proofing your house and being vigilant about how you store household products after you use them is very important. In the sections that follow, we outline the most common household hazards.

Preventing poisoning from foods and medications

Not all foods that taste good to you are good for your dog. Some, if eaten in enough quantity, can even kill your canine companion. The toxic foods discussed here are the ones deemed most dangerous to dogs by the National Animal Poison Control Center.

For some of these toxic foods, I have provided *approximate* amounts that are toxic, but avoid feeding *any* of these foods to your dog, even in small amounts.

- **Onions:** A toxic component of raw onions can cause the red blood cells to burst, resulting in severe anemia and even kidney failure. A medium-sized raw onion can cause illness in a 40-pound dog.
- **Chocolate, cocoa, coffee, or tea:** Chocolate, coffee, and tea all contain caffeine and theobromine. These toxins can cause vomiting, diarrhea, increased thirst, hyperactivity, increased heart rate, and even seizures. The toxic dose of milk chocolate is 1 ounce per kilogram of body weight, which translates to about 1½ pounds of milk chocolate for a 50-pound dog.
- **Alcohol (ethanol):** Alcohol can cause vomiting, staggering, weakness, and even coma in dogs. One ounce of ethanol (100-percent alcohol) is enough to cause illness in a 65-pound dog.
- **Yeast dough:** There are two problems associated with ingestion of yeast dough. The first problem is that the yeast can ferment and produce alcohol, producing the same illness as alcohol toxicity. The second problem is that the yeast can swell in a dog's stomach and cause obstruction or even rupture of the stomach.
- **Salt:** Salt can cause illness in a dog, especially if the dog doesn't have access to water. Dogs with salt toxicity stagger and wander aimlessly, eventually developing seizures that progress to a coma and death.
- **Macadamia nuts:** About 10 ounces of macadamia nuts can cause soreness, stiffness, listlessness, and rear leg weakness in dogs.
- **Green or unripe tomatoes or potatoes and their leaves and stems:** The level of toxicity of these vegetables and

their plant parts depends very much on the soil, the temperature and humidity when they are grown. They can cause slowing or complete cessation of digestion, increased heart rate, and signs of excitability such as shaking, panting and pacing. If you are feeding fresh greens to your dog, make sure these items aren't included.

- **Moldy foods:** Moldy foods can have a variety of toxic fungi and bacteria growing in them. Never give old food from the refrigerator to your dog.

Never let your dog have access to decaying garbage or road kill. Rotting meat is contaminated with bacteria and toxins produced by bacteria that can be toxic to your dog. Keep your dog properly confined at home and store your garbage in an area to which your dog does not have access.

Animal poisoning by drugs is very common, accounting for over 75 percent of toxin exposures reported by animal poison control centers. Never give human prescription or over-the-counter medications to your dog unless specifically prescribed by your veterinarian, and keep all drugs out of your dog's reach. Many human medications are lethal to dogs, even in small doses. Here are some of the most common toxic human medications that dogs get into:

- Analgesic and anti-inflammatory drugs (aspirin, ibuprofen, acetaminophen, naproxen)
- Antidepressants
- Cold medicine or decongestants
- Creams and ointments in tubes
- Diet pills
- Vitamins

Keeping chemicals out of your dog's reach

Many household chemicals are toxic if ingested by animals. Cleaning materials can cause digestive upsets if your dog eats them. Some products, such as those containing lye, can cause burns to the mouth. Here are the most common dangerous household items that contain chemicals:

- Batteries
- Cigarettes
- Dishwashing detergent
- Fabric softener sheets
- Moth balls
- Potpourri oils

Like household cleaning solutions, car cleaning compounds are also toxic. In fact, frequently they are more dangerous because they are more concentrated. Antifreeze is extremely toxic to dogs; less than 1 tablespoon can kill a 10-pound dog. Windshield washer fluid is also toxic, though less so. Restrict your dog's access to the garage as much as possible, so you can ensure that your dog stays away from these dangerous items.

All the insecticides you might have around your home are potentially toxic to your canine companion. Almost all topical anti-flea preparations (dips and sprays) are toxic to dogs, given enough exposure. When applying a flea-control product to your dog, be sure to use it *exactly* as recommended and apply it directly to the dog's skin. When using household insecticides, read the label carefully and use the product exactly as recommended.

Mouse and rat poisons are highly toxic to dogs. After all, they are designed to kill small animals. Try to avoid chemicals whenever you can: Try a mousetrap rather than poison, beer rather than slug bait, nonchemical lawn products rather than chemical ones — and only go to the chemical weapons if all else fails.

Keep insecticides and poisonous animal bait out of areas your dog frequents and remove them when they are no longer needed.

Never use garden or lawn care chemicals in the presence of your dog. Keep your dog away when you apply fertilizers to help your roses grow and your grass stay green throughout the summer.

I use the "double-safe" rule for storing toxic products in the home. First, I store the items in a room to which my dogs are forbidden access. Plus, I store the items in a location within that room (for example, high on a shelf) that my dogs couldn't reach if they were somehow able to get into the room.

Chapter 3

Housetraining Your Canine Companion

In This Chapter

- Preparing for housetraining
- Training your dog to potty outside
- Preventing and troubleshooting accidents

Most people who choose to live with dogs want to be able to regulate their canines' bathroom deportment. They want their dogs to poop and pee where and when *they* (the people) choose. Why does such precision matter? Simple: An otherwise well-behaved, healthy dog who doesn't know proper pooch potty protocol is much more likely to lose her home than a similar dog who knows her bathroom basics.

The way you teach your dog the proper potty protocol lays the foundation for your efforts to teach her other maneuvers, like sitting when told to or coming when called (see Chapter 4 for more on those manners). What you do now, in this most basic of lessons, can set the tone for your relationship with your dog in the years ahead. This chapter helps you prepare for housetraining, shows you how to housetrain your dog successfully, and provides pointers for dealing with bathroom accidents.

Planning a Potty Strategy

Before you can start housetraining your puppy or adult dog, you must do some prep work. To be successful at housetraining, your dog needs a crate, and you need to understand how your dog views her crate. We also tell you how your doggie's dining habits affect her bathroom behaviors.

Considering a crate's benefits

Professional dog trainers and experienced dog owners have dealt with a lot of puppy pee and doggie doo. Not surprisingly, they've gotten housetraining down to a science. And just about every one of them will tell you that using a crate makes housetraining easier, quicker, and more effective than any other method.

"A crate?" you ask. "How can that be? They look like cages, not potty-training devices." Looks, however, can be deceiving. Crates are unquestionably the way to go if you want your dog to become a housetraining ace as soon as possible. (For more on crates, flip to Chapter 2.)

Few objects are more important to a wild or domestic canine than the den — that safe, secure place that the animal can call his own. A crate makes a perfect doggie den. It's compact, it's cozy, and it's dark inside (or you can render it so by draping a towel or blanket atop the crate). And because a crate is open on one side but enclosed on the other three, it offers the dog a safe, secure window through which he can watch his world.

Dogs who are introduced to the crate at a young age soon grow to love their special spaces, and an older dog can learn to at least tolerate a crate when introduced to one properly. Either way, the attachment is worth cultivating because doing so enables you to tap into a crucial component of your canine companion's denning instinct.

Instinctively, a normal, healthy dog will do just about anything to avoid having to use his den as a toilet area. The last thing he wants to do is deposit his bodily waste anywhere near his cherished domicile. You can make that impulse work in your favor as you housetrain your dog. The impulse to keep the den clean is the cornerstone to teaching dogs to poop and pee only where and when you want them to. The drive to use a den and the drive to avoid soiling that den form the basis of easy, effective housetraining using a crate.

How long can a dog hold it?

Some dogs appear to have bladders made of iron. Co-author Susan's late, great Sheltie, Cory, was one such canine. When the weather was bad, he slapped his floodgates shut. His personal best was a whopping 23 hours, even though Susan gave him ample opportunity to unload during that time period.

Still, just because your dog has an iron bladder doesn't mean you should put it to the test. Here are some guidelines:

- Most experts say a dog needs a chance to pee at least every eight to ten hours.
- For puppies, the standard guideline is that they can hold it for the number of months they've lived plus one. In other words, your 3-month-old youngster can hold it for about four hours, max. But for many puppies of that age, even four hours is pushing their anatomical limits; they may need trips every three hours or even every two hours for a while.
- Very small puppies, such as toy breeds, often need hourly potty breaks when they're under 4 months of age simply because their bladders are so small.

Knowing how feeding and watering affect housetraining

What comes out of your dog in the form of pee or poop is directly related to what you put into him. Consequently, if you control what you feed your four-legged friend, you also exert some control over his bathroom behavior. That what-goes-in-eventually-comes-out principle of housetraining manifests itself in countless ways. Here are just a few examples:

- **What you feed:** This affects the size and consistency of your dog's poop, as well as how often he may need to do the doo. For example, if your dog eats a lot of vegetables, he'll probably need to poop more often than the pooch who prefers more basic canine fare. Vegetables contain relatively high amounts of fiber, and fiber acts as a laxative.

  Also, food that's high in salt is likely to make your dog thirsty. Ingesting goodies that have a lot of salt in them, such as many table scraps, may send your pooch to his water dish more often. And the more times your dog tanks up, the more often he's going to need to empty his tank (his bladder).

Even different types of dog food affect your dog's bathroom output. A dog who eats a raw food diet tends to have firmer, more compact stools than a pooch whose diet consists of other fare.

- **When you feed:** Timing directly affects when your dog needs to potty. A canine housetrainee who eats his dinner at 5 p.m. needs a post-dinner pit stop earlier in the evening than the dog who sups at 7 p.m.
- **How you feed:** A pooch who has to gulp his food amid a chaotic atmosphere may suffer from an upset stomach — which in turn can result in more frequent, looser, and tougher-to-clean-up bowel movements.

Understanding How Outdoor Training Works

Outdoor training is the process of teaching your dog to eliminate only when he's outside. You can consider your pooch to be successfully outdoor-trained if she consistently holds her poop and pee until you take her outside — or if she takes herself there.

Achieving such success can be surprisingly simple. Every time you think your dog needs a potty break, you take her outside to her potty spot to do her business. At first, you do this according to a set schedule. Sometimes, though, your dog needs to diverge from that schedule — and in all likelihood, she'll communicate somehow that she needs to go.

At all other times, you either confine her to her crate or watch her continuously for those pre-potty communications. The objectives here are to prevent accidents from occurring and to encourage your dog to do her business outdoors — and outdoors only. Within a matter of weeks, she understands that it's okay to potty outside and takes it upon herself to make sure that she doesn't eliminate inside.

Outdoor training needn't be difficult, but it does require time, attention, and patience from you. Training puppies takes a little more work than training an adult dog — for one thing, puppies need more potty breaks — but either way, you can introduce your dog to her potty spot, set up a schedule, and get training off to a good start.

Training Your Pooch to Go Potty Outdoors

The great thing about outdoor training is that you can start doing it right away. And if you're really lucky, your dog's breeder has started the process for you. In the following sections, you find out how to encourage your dog with verbal cues and how to develop a training schedule.

A good potty spot is any place that's fairly close to your house and easy to clean. Plan to clean up your dog's potty area at least once a day.

Teaching proper potty protocol

The way you behave while your puppy potties can either speed up or slow down his outdoor housetraining progress. That's because puppies have very short attention spans, and they can have a hard time staying focused during their potty breaks. Your behavior can either help your little guy get down to business or make him forget to do his business.

Teaching an adult dog to do his bathroom business outside is similar to teaching a puppy. The difference between the two is that the adult dog doesn't need nearly as many bathroom breaks as a puppy does. But the principles and procedures are the same: showing your four-legged friend that his bathroom is outside and doing whatever it takes to keep him from eliminating inside.

Going out to the potty spot

To help your puppy concentrate on bathroom activities, get him thinking about those activities before you reach the potty spot. As the two of you head out to your pup's bathroom, ask him, "Do you want to go potty?" or announce to him, "It's potty time!" in a lively, can't-wait-to-get-out-there tone. Use the same expression and same tone of voice every time you take Fido out, and soon he'll associate both with heading out to the bathroom.

Take the fastest, most direct route to the potty area and use the same route every time your dog needs a bathroom break. Your consistency conditions Fido to expect that when he treads that path, he's going to eliminate shortly thereafter.

As you go to the potty spot, make sure you don't walk him near the mailbox or your prize rhododendron. The dog shouldn't be allowed to pee just anywhere, particularly in the housetraining process. Even after your dog is housetrained, keep him off other people's lawns and confine his bathroom activities to the median strip between the sidewalk and street when you go for walks.

Letting your pup do his business

When the two of you arrive at the potty spot, don't do anything. Don't talk to your dog and don't play with him until he's figured out where he's going to go and is clearly about to do so. Let him walk around a little bit — no farther than the length of a 6-foot leash — and don't let him leave the area until he's unloaded.

As your little guy squats (male puppies don't start lifting their legs to pee until they're older, and most females never do), give him a command such as "Go potty" or "Do your business." Repeat this phrase every time he eliminates. By doing so, you up your puppy's chances of learning to pee and poop on command — a handy skill for him to have.

As soon as your pup is finished, praise him for his performance in a high, happy-sounding voice. Give him a small treat immediately after he does his good deed so he associates the reward with the deed. Then take him for a walk, play with him, and indulge in a love fest. You've both earned it!

A matter of timing: Setting up a potty schedule

Your dog is a creature of habit. He learns through repetition. If you take him out to pee and poop at the same times each and every day, his body will become accustomed to that schedule. He'll be conditioned to do his business at the times you want him to do it.

A regular potty schedule also eases your job as your dog's caregiver. That's because a change in a dog's regular bathroom behavior often signals that he's sick. But if your dog potties unpredictably, you won't be able to pick up any such signals.

During your puppy's first few days at home, you should note — preferably in writing — when he goes and whether he poops, pees, or does both. You're likely to see a pattern emerge that can help you anticipate when your new family member needs to eliminate. You can use that knowledge to create a sleeping, feeding, and bathroom schedule to help your four-legged friend become a housetraining expert in a surprisingly short time.

When you put together a potty schedule for your puppy, keep in mind that most juvenile canines need to poop and/or pee at the following times:

- First thing in the morning
- Last thing at night
- During the night (if the puppy is under 4 months of age)
- After energetic playing
- After being confined in a crate
- After a nap
- After chewing on a toy or a bone
- A few minutes after eating

Armed with this knowledge, along with your observations of your dog's individual potty pattern, you can create a schedule that gives your puppy enough time to pee or poop and also gives you some predictability. Table 3-1 shows how you may structure a schedule for a 3-month-old pup. Note that all trips outside are just to the potty spot — the puppy should come inside after he's finished unloading. Note, too, that puppies younger than 3 months are likely to need go out more often.

Table 3-1 Outdoor Training Schedule for a 3-Month-Old Puppy

Time	*Tasks*
7:00 a.m.	Take puppy outside. Feed puppy. Offer water. Take puppy outside. Play with puppy up to 15 minutes. Take puppy outside. Put puppy in crate.
Midmorning	Take puppy outside. Offer water. Play with puppy up to 15 minutes. Take puppy outside. Put puppy in crate.
Noon	Take puppy outside. Feed puppy. Offer water. Take puppy outside. Play with puppy 15 to 30 minutes. Take puppy outside. Put puppy in crate.
Midafternoon	Take puppy outside. Offer water. Play with puppy up to 15 minutes. Take puppy outside. Put puppy in crate.
5:30 p.m.	Take puppy outside. Feed puppy. Offer water. Take puppy outside. Play with puppy up to 1 hour and/or let him hang out with the family in the kitchen.
7:00 p.m.	Take puppy outside. Play with puppy up to 15 minutes. Put puppy in crate.
Before bed	Take puppy outside. Put puppy in crate.
During the night	Take puppy outside if necessary.

Know that as your puppy gets older, he won't need to go outside in the middle of the night. The same will be true of the midmorning, midafternoon, and early evening pit stops, as well as the noontime feeding. Think twice, though, about giving him unsupervised freedom in your house, even if he's completely housetrained.

Table 3-2 shows a sample schedule for outdoor-training an adult dog. As soon as your adult dog has mastered her housetraining basics — which can happen in just a few days — you can eliminate the noontime potty break and consider giving her a little more freedom in your home.

Table 3-2 Outdoor Training Schedule for an Adult Dog

Time	*Tasks*
7:00 a.m.	Get up. Take dog outside. Feed dog. Offer water. Take dog outside. Play with dog up to 15 minutes. Put dog in crate.
Noon	Take dog outside. Offer water. Play with dog 15 to 30 minutes. Put dog in crate.
5:30 p.m.	Take dog outside. Feed dog. Offer water. Play with dog for 1 hour and/or let him hang out with the family in the kitchen.
7:00 p.m.	Remove water.
Before bed	Take dog outside. Put dog in crate.

Dealing with Oopsies

Yes, we know: Your puppy or dog is the most wonderful creature ever to have graced the planet (aside from yourself, your spouse, and your kids). But alas, even this paragon is not perfect; she makes mistakes — and many occur during the housetraining process. Despite your best efforts to teach her bathroom manners, your four-legged friend may not understand immediately what she's supposed to do or not do. She'll demonstrate that lack of understanding by pooping or peeing inside your home instead of outside in her designated potty area.

In the following sections, we tell you how to respond to bathroom boo-boos, whether you spot your dog in a squat or find a puddle or pile already on the floor.

Catching your dog in the act

If you come upon your four-legged friend starting to perform that unmistakable potty squat, you have a superb teachable moment. Your objective here: Divert your dog from doing the doo in the wrong place and put her in a position to do it in the right place.

Distract your dog from making the wrong move by offering a tiny treat or a toy, clapping your hands, or saying "Oops!" in a cheerful voice. As you do so, hustle her outside to her potty spot as quickly as possible so she can finish what she started but do so in the right place. After she unloads there, praise her lavishly and give her a couple of additional treats.

Finding messes: Don't scold — just clean 'em up!

Potty mistakes try the soul of even the most patient dog owner. But no matter how irritated you feel, it's crucial to the success of your housetraining venture not to take your frustration out on your outdoor trainee. Take a deep breath and remind yourself that any mistakes she makes are *not* her fault, and don't scold her in any way. Instead, take your little transgressor back to her crate so you can concentrate on cleanup, but don't say anything to her.

After your four-legged friend is safely confined in her doggie den, grab some paper towels and some pet stain remover. Follow the directions on the cleaner bottle and clean up the evidence of your puppy's doo-doo boo-boo. Take her out when you've cleaned up completely, have calmed down, and can watch her.

Please, please, please don't try to correct your erring pooch by scolding her, punishing her, or rubbing her nose in her transgression. Any after-the-fact corrective efforts will be lost on her.

Folded-down ears, a tail between the legs, and a refusal to look at you do not indicate that your dog feels bad about her bathroom boo-boo. The body language you're seeing shows that she feels uneasy, distressed, or maybe even scared because of the body language that you're exhibiting. But guilty? Nope.

So if your dog doesn't understand what she's done and doesn't feel any guilt, what should you do? Simple: Just clean up the mess. Then figure out where you went wrong, as we explain in the next section.

Preventing further accidents

After you clean up a pile or puddle, think about what happened and who should take the blame for your four-legged friend's mistake. Here's a hint: Instead of focusing on your dog, focus on yourself. If she peed in your living room, ask yourself what she was doing in the living room unattended in the first place. If she pooped on your kitchen floor, ask yourself when her last bowel movement was and whether you should've anticipated that by getting her outside earlier. In other words, try to figure out what you could've done to prevent your dog's accident and what you can do to make sure that she doesn't do an encore. Table 3-3 can help you get started.

Table 3-3 Troubleshooting Your Dog's Accident

What Your Dog Did	*What You Can Do*
She peed when your back was turned.	Never let her out of her crate or living area unless you're prepared to watch her every minute.
She peed or pooped in her crate.	Make sure her crate isn't too big for her; it should be just large enough for her to stand up and turn around. Make sure, too, that she's not left in the crate for too long — three to four hours, max.
She pooped without warning.	Observe what she does immediately before she makes a deposit. That way, you'll be able to scoop her up and take her outside before she has an accident.
She pees on the same indoor spot daily.	Make sure you clean up completely. And don't give your dog too much indoor freedom too soon.

Any canine potty accident contains a lesson — but the lesson is for you, not your dog. By figuring out where you went wrong and making sure that you don't make the same mistake again, you'll make a giant leap toward having a truly housetrained dog.

Chapter 4

Communicating and Teaching Basic Manners

In This Chapter

- Speaking your dog's language
- Teaching your dog basic commands

The most important factor in training is not your dog, but *you.* You're the leader — or you should be — and you need to know enough about canine language so you can teach your dog *your* language. You need to show your dog what you want her to do and give her a reason for doing it — and an understanding that not doing the very reasonable things you ask of her is unacceptable.

Your dog gets trained, whether you do anything or not. If you don't guide her toward good behaviors and praise her when she accomplishes them, she will fill her life with behaviors you don't like. If you don't lead, she will.

In this chapter, we show you how to communicate with your pup. Then you can train her to be the dog of your dreams — without too much work.

DogSpeak 101: Figuring Out How to Communicate with Your Pet

Communication is the give and take of information. Every relationship needs good communication, including the relationships we have with our dogs. In fact, an essential part of training your dog is knowing how to communicate with him. If you can figure that out, you're on your way to having a well-trained companion.

In the following sections, we tell you how to communicate with your dog, tell you how your dog interprets what you say, and give you some tips for communicating better.

Knowing how your dog communicates

Body language is the language of dogs. Because they speak body language, dogs also are great observers. Your dog reads slight shifts in your posture and the position of your arms, legs, and hands. He observes the position of your eyebrows, the turn of your mouth, and the expression in your eyes. From all this information he understands your likes, your dislikes, your needs, your wants, your moods, and your thoughts.

Try this experiment, and you'll discover how observant your dog is. Next time your canine friend disobeys you, don't say anything. Instead, put your hands on your hips and frown. Your brows should be furrowed, your eyes angry, and your mouth down-turned. Your dog will get the message that you aren't happy with his behavior, even though you haven't spoken a word.

Even though our dogs are always observing (or listening to) us, we frequently are not very good at listening to them, mainly because we're much more dependent on verbal language. If you take a little time to learn the canine language, however, you'll reap the rewards of a stronger bond with your dog.

The key to the canine language is that dogs use a combination of body posture, facial expression, and tail position to represent phrases. To be fully versed in the canine language, you need to observe *all* parts of your dog's body. If you concentrate only on one part, such as the tail or the face, you may make a significant language blunder.

Table 4-1 lists a few of the most common canine phrases. As you become a better observer, you'll become quite fluent in the canine language:

Table 4-1 Translating between English and DogSpeak

English	*DogSpeak*
I'm happy.	Ears relaxed, tail wagging gently, head held high.
I'm ecstatic!	Ears floppy, tail wagging vigorously, rear end wiggling with effort.
Let's play!	Ears forward but relaxed, eyes bright and teasing, lips pulled back slightly but relaxed, tail up.
Who's that?	Ears erect and forward, eyes wide open, neck outstretched, tail still.
I'm afraid.	Ears back but stiff, tail tucked under, head down, eyes closed a little and shifting back and forth.
Watch out or I'll bite!	Ears forward and stiff, lips raised exposing teeth, hair on shoulders raised, tip of tail lashing back and forth.

Be careful of dogs who show signs of fear. Many more dogs bite because of fear than because of aggression. Learn to read the warning signs that show a dog is afraid, especially when you're meeting a new dog. If you see signs of fear or aggression, give that dog a wide berth.

Reinforcing good behavior and correcting the bad

Just as with kids, you won't get very far with your dog if all you ever do is yell at him when he's done something wrong, and he won't learn what's wrong if all you ever do is praise him when he's done something right. Training is a delicate balance between praising good behavior and correcting bad behavior.

Do that again!: Letting your dog know when he's on the right track

Your dog will learn more easily if you teach him a specific word that means that he's right. You can use any word such as "Nice," "Great," "Yes," or "Good" to communicate to your dog that he's done what you wanted. Choose a one-syllable word that doesn't sound like your dog's name and won't be confused with a command word such as "Sit" or "Down." We use "Yes" as an example in this section, but you can substitute a word of your choosing.

Start by showing your dog that when you say "Yes!" you mean, "What you just did is right." The best way to help your dog make that connection is with food. Essentially, you'll be making a link in your dog's mind between the food and the word "Yes!" With a few treats in your hand, say "Yes!" and then immediately give your dog a treat. Repeat this exercise eight to ten times, making sure that your dog isn't always in the same position (so he knows it's not that particular position you're rewarding) and that he isn't barking, jumping up, or doing anything else you don't want to reward. Over the next few days, repeat this exercise in different locations both in the house and outside. When you see that your dog perks up (expecting food) when you say "Yes!" you'll know he understands the meaning of the word. Now you have a tool you can use in training to mark the correct behavior. You don't have to have food always at the ready. You can just say "Yes!"

Stop right there!: Being sure your dog knows what's bad in your book

To give your dog the complete picture of what correct behavior is, you need to let him know when he's doing the wrong thing. This is called *correction.* A correction is something that makes your dog want to stop a behavior. One of the best ways to correct your dog is to say "At!" Although it may not make a whole lot of sense to say the word "at" as a correction, most dogs instinctively dislike the sound, and that's all that matters.

Show your dog exactly what "At!" means by putting a treat in the palm of your hand and showing it to your dog. If he tries to get the food, say "At!" and close your hand around the food. Look away, ignoring him. Then try again. If he sits still, waiting for you to give the word, say "Yes!" because he's got it! Just as you will say "Yes!" when your dog is doing something right, you now can say "At!" when he's doing something wrong. This is the foundation of teaching your dog right from wrong.

Physical punishment rarely lets any dog know the difference between right and wrong. Unless you can be right beside your dog at the second he makes the mistake, chances are that, by the time you strike him, he will have moved on to another behavior and will have no idea why you've just hit him. Plus, some dogs react aggressively to physical punishment.

Are you concerned that you may hurt your dog's feelings by verbally correcting him? If so, keep in mind that dogs are much happier when all the rules are clear and everything is black and white. Uncertainty makes dogs unhappy; so it stands to reason that knowing what *not* to do is as important as knowing what *to* do. And this is the purpose of corrections.

Putting it all together

So how do you use reinforcement and correction together to train your dog? Here we use training your dog to sit as an example.

1. **Arm yourself with an ample supply of treats and toys.**

   Fanny packs are great for holding treats. They allow you to carry more than you can in your hand. Plus, they keep the treats out of your dog's sight.

2. **With your dog standing beside or in front of you, and while holding his collar gently, position a treat slightly above your dog's head and move the treat slowly backward.**

   This causes your dog to raise his head and lower his rear to follow the food. Holding his collar prevents him from jumping up for the food.

3. **As soon as your dog sits, say "Yes!" and give him the treat.**

   You have just reinforced that good behavior.

4. **Repeat this exercise four or five times.**

   Before long, your dog probably will be plopping his butt down as soon as you get a piece of food out of your fanny pack. That's because he already has made an association between his behavior and its consequences (food). Give him a few more short lessons over the next week or so, saying "Yes!" and giving him a treat each time he sits.

5. **Next time you play this game, say "Sit" as you place the food above his head. Continue to say "Yes!" and give him a treat when he sits.**

   This exercise teaches your dog that he should perform the behavior not just when you hold the food above his head, but also when you say "Sit."

6. **When you're sure your dog knows what the word "Sit!" means, start giving him the treat randomly, not every time you ask him to sit.**

   You don't need to give your dog a treat each time he sits after he has learned the behavior. Studies have shown a dog is more likely to obey a command if he doesn't know whether he'll be reinforced or not. Be sure to always praise him, however, even if you don't give him a treat.

At some point, your little Einstein will ignore your request to sit. At this point, you need to show him that ignoring you isn't an option. It's time for you to administer a correction:

1. **Take his collar and gently and unemotionally pull up and back to move him into a sitting position.**
2. **When he is sitting, say "Yes!"**
3. **Move him and ask him to sit again.**

   If he sits, say "Yes!" and give him a treat. He'll respect you for insisting and will be more likely to comply next time.

How do you know when your dog needs correcting? When he makes mistakes but is still learning your command, use only rewards. After he completely understands a command, you can correct him if he is distracted or deliberately refuses to obey.

Training the Polite Pooch

Your dog will be happier and healthier if you appreciate and love him, and that's easier to do when your dog is familiar with basic obedience training. Your pooch will know how you expect him to behave, and you'll spend less time saying, "No." In the following sections, we present the basic manners that well-mannered dogs know. When you're ready to get started, make sure you have a suitable collar and leash for your dog (see Chapter 2) and plenty of treats to reward your pup's positive actions.

Deliver commands in a sensible, no-nonsense tone, loudly and clearly enough for your dog to hear — but never yell. Don't whine a command, and don't say it angrily or rough. Give the command as if you expect it to be obeyed and are confident that it will be.

How often should you train your dog? When you're trying to introduce something new, short lessons twice a day are ideal. You don't have to teach everything at once. Just do the "Sit," twice a day for a week, if that's all you have time for. Then train the "Down," and so on. Just be consistent. If you take up the same lesson for a day or two and then drop it for two weeks, you'll never get anywhere. After your dog knows the command, look for every opportunity to practice and praise.

"Sit"

To teach "Sit," you take the slack out of the leash with your right hand, but don't tighten it. Offer a treat slightly over and behind your dog's head, with your right hand, and give the command "Sit." He might sit just from being off balance, and if he does, praise and treat. If not, spread the index finger and thumb of your left hand and place them on either side of your dog, just in front of his hip bone, with the underside of your finger and thumb resting on his back. Say "Sit" and exert gentle pressure inward and down. He should fold up to avoid the pressure, and when he does, praise and treat.

"Down"

"Down" builds on "Sit," so make sure your dog understands that behavior first. Start with the dog sitting at your left side with the slack taken out of the leash. Give the command "Down," and use a treat to guide your pet into position, drawing the treat between his legs and forward. When he's in position, give him the treat and praise.

"Stay"

"Stay" is a command used in conjunction with another command, a request of your dog to hold whatever position you put him in, whether it's "Sit," "Down," or "Rest on the couch." After your dog learns "Stay" in relation to one position, applying the command to the other positions is pretty easy.

Start with the "Sit," and with the dog at your side, hold the leash in a straight line up from his head with all the slack out. Flash an open palm in front of your dog's nose (hand signals work especially well with this command) and then say "Stay."

Step out in front of your dog so you can block his forward motion. If he moves, flash your hand and repeat the "Stay" command. If he stays, return to your position alongside him, and after a second or two, praise and treat, and then release him and praise him again.

From there, you want to build up time and distances in slow increments. When you're working at the end of the 6-foot leash and your dog is staying reliably, tug on the leash a little without making a sound. If he moves, go back and correct him verbally, repeat the command sequence, and try it again. When he resists the tug, return to position alongside him, praise, and then release him.

"Heel"

"Heel" teaches your dog to walk calmly at your side, instead of dragging you down the street. To teach "Heel," your dog should be sitting on your left. Call his name, say "Heel" and step off on your left leg so he can see that you're leaving. Praise him for leaving and for staying alongside. If he darts forward, however, turn and head in the other direction, repeating "Heel," and praising and treating him for responding. Keep your dog focused on you and keep praising and treating for trying. When you stop, ask your dog to "Sit" at your side. Eventually, that "Sit" becomes automatic.

"Come"

Teaching "Come" is easy. Put your dog on a "Sit-Stay" on leash, call his name, say "Come," reel him in with praise, and give more praise and treats when he gets to you. Train your dog to "Come" in increments, on-leash and on longer leashes. Try "Come" in different places, too: in the house, in the yard, in the park, with your kids playing. Never let him get into a position where he learns you really can't do much about it when he bolts. Practice, not just in formal training but in everyday life. Don't forget the treats, and don't forget the praise.

If your untrained dog slips out and takes off, try to use a command he knows well — like "Sit" — instead of "Come." This is an emergency after all — a wrong move and he could be road pizza. Most dogs know "Sit" so well they'll plant their rumps and, after they're planted, you can praise and take their collars.

Chapter 5

Day-to-Day Care for Your Dog

In This Chapter

- Choosing the best food for your dog
- Staying fit with dog-friendly exercise
- Grooming for a great look

Just like you have a daily routine of meals, grooming, and activity, your dog needs the same. Quality food will keep her body in working order; a dose of daily exercise will keep her bones strong; and frequent brushing, bathing, and trimming will keep her looking sharp. This chapter covers what you need to do on a regular basis to make the most of your relationship with your canine pal.

Fulfilling Basic Nutritional Needs

About 60 nutritional elements go into keeping your pet healthy, all working together to keep his body working as it should be. These nutrients each play a role, and although some seem to have a bigger part than others, each is necessary to keep your dog's body functioning. I touch on each of the main canine nutrition needs in the following sections.

When you're reading labels, you may notice that the percentages don't add up to 100. That's because the labels record the percentages of the food that are nutritionally available to the animal. Whatever isn't usable is what comes out the other end, as waste. That's why food with higher-quality ingredients usually produces less to clean up in the yard.

Protein

Dog food contains healthy levels of protein — from 14 to 21 percent of their diet for older dogs, to 25 to 42 percent for growing dogs or dogs who still put in a full day's work, such as herding dogs or sled dogs.

Protein provides *amino acids,* which your dog reassembles into the protein parts of his body — his own flesh, for example. All animals require these life-giving nutrients. Some amino acids, called *nonessential,* are synthesized in the dog's body; others, called *essential,* must be obtained from food. Variety and quality are the important things to remember when considering protein sources. A combination of meat, poultry, fish, dairy products, and other sources of protein ensures that your dog is getting all the essential amino acids he needs in his diet.

Carbohydrates

Carbohydrates — sugars and starches — are a source of energy. Of all the ingredients in prepared dog foods, carbohydrates are probably not what a dog would choose to eat in the wild — although as opportunistic eaters, they take what they can find.

Dogs are able to use the carbohydrates found in commercial foods, and that's a good thing, because by weight these carbs are the largest component of most commercial dog foods.

Fats

In our society, we worry endlessly about the amount of fat in our diets, which experts say is too high. Dogs often consume more fat than they should, also. But don't go crazy cutting it out — fats are an important part of a dog's diet (and your diet, too).

Fat is essential for the absorption and movement around the body of fat-soluble vitamins. Fat also provides food with much of its appeal to the canine nose and palate, and with essential fatty acids which play an important role in coat quality.

Vitamins and minerals

Vitamins are divided into two categories — *water-soluble* and *fat-soluble.* Both are important to your dog's health, and the lack of any vitamin in your pet's diet can have dire effects. Water-soluble vitamins include the B vitamins, niacin, panthothenic acid, folic acid, biotin, choline, and vitamin C. Fat-soluble vitamins are vitamins A, D, E, and K.

Mineral nutrients your dog needs include potassium, magnesium, zinc, calcium, iron, phosphorus, sodium, chloride, and others. Like vitamins, they make up a small part of your pet's diet, but they're essential for good health.

The important thing to know about vitamins and minerals is that your dog needs the correct amount — but not more. "If a little is good, a lot must be better" simply doesn't apply in the case of vitamins — and nearly all other nutrients. An oversupply of vitamins and minerals can prove dangerous, which is why you should not give your pet supplements unless you've discussed it with your veterinarian first.

Water

Do you think about nutrition as just being what your dog eats? Don't forget that what your pet drinks is just as important to her well-being. Water — clean, fresh, and ever-present — is essential to nearly every process of your dog's body, which is, after all, composed of 70 percent water.

The tiniest cells of living beings cannot survive without water. Nutrients are carried and wastes removed by water. A dog can go without eating for weeks if need be (please don't test this fact, though), but without water, death comes in days.

Choosing Food for Fido

You could perform hours of research on all the ingredients in dog food. Whole books are available on the subject; you could go to the library at your closest school or college of veterinary medicine and lose yourself in the stacks for days.

You don't need to go to such lengths, however, to make sure your dog's eating right. You can do just fine if you follow some simple guidelines:

- **Choose brands that are appropriate for your dog's age, breed, and condition.** Look for the words "Complete and

Balanced Nutrition" on the label, as well as the Association of American Feed Control Officials (AAFCO) animal-feeding tested statement "for all life stages." Talk to your veterinarian about what food is appropriate for your dog, especially when it comes to levels of protein and fat.

- **Choose brands from major manufacturers.** Whether you buy your dog's food from the supermarket, a pet-supply store, or your veterinarian, as long as you're dealing with a major manufacturer's food that carries the "AAFCO animal tested" statement, you should be fine.

Should you pop the extra dough for more expensive premium foods? That's up to you. Some owners like them because they often contain higher quality, more digestible ingredients that are more easily absorbed. These foods often require less volume — both going in and coming out. But other than that, the fact is these diets offer no proven health advantage.

Ask your veterinarian for a recommendation, and stick to it after you're satisfied it's working well for your dog and that he likes it. Dogs don't need variety, and they don't get bored with the same ration day after day. When a healthy dog is a picky eater, it's usually because the owners taught him to be that way, by adding tempting tidbits at the least sign of reluctance to eat.

Checking out meal options

The food-processing industry, so busy providing convenient foods for the human population, also is active in manufacturing affordable, convenient food for pets. The commercially available choices for your dog's main diet are

- **Dry food:** Also called kibble, this variety comes in a box or a bag, and is the least expensive. Dry food helps reduce tartar buildup on your pet's teeth. Dogs generally aren't as crazy about dry food, however, as they are about freshly opened canned food.
- **Canned foods:** Ranging from meat-and-meal diets to preparations meant to be mixed with kibble, this stuff is loved by dogs. It's expensive to feed because you're paying for a lot of water. It also becomes unattractive quickly if left to stand by a dog who is a less voracious eater. Canned food can be great for nursing ill or older dogs, however, especially those whose teeth make dry food hard to handle.

- **Semi-moist foods:** This is a more recent development, often designed to look like people food — hamburger patties or sausage. Sort of a midway point between dry and canned in terms of ease of use and cost, semi-moist foods are often criticized for appealing more to humans — with clever shapes and artificial colors — than to dogs.

Most dogs do fine on a steady diet of kibble, with nothing at all added.

How much food, and when?

The label provides a guideline on the amount of food recommended for your dog. It's just a start, though. Dogs who are highly active, pregnant, or are nursing puppies have higher energy requirements than the average canine. In the wintertime, indoor dogs often need less food because they're less active, while outdoor dogs need more because staying warm burns calories.

A good guideline is to feed two-thirds of the daily ration in the morning and the remaining one-third in the evening. Because dogs have a tendency to sleep after meals, this technique is especially useful for animals who have to stay alone all day — a sleepy dog is less likely to chew or bark.

Some people can get away with letting the dog decide when and how much he eats. Keeping a constant supply of kibble available (known as *free-feeding*) works in some cases, usually in single-dog households where there's no competition for food.

If you find your pet can maintain his own weight and you aren't having related behavioral problems like house-soiling, then free-feeding is fine. But realize that you won't be able to pick up on subtle changes in your pet's eating habits that may be an early indicator of health problems. You also won't be able to use giving your dog food — after he sits — as an effortless way to reinforce your role as pack leader.

Treating Your Dog

Giving your pet a little something special from time to time isn't going to do him any harm and can be very useful in training situations, or when you're trying to keep him occupied while he's home alone. Here are a couple things to keep in mind, however:

- **All things in moderation.** Treats, whether store-bought or from your dinner plate, don't make a good diet for your pet. Make sure the majority of his food doesn't come from extra goodies.
- **Avoid some foods entirely.** Food that's heavily spiced or fatty can upset your dog's digestion, leading to diarrhea, vomiting, or even a life-threatening ailment such as pancreatitis.
- **Think before you treat.** If you give your dog treats from your plate, you can't complain that he's a pest at mealtime. And if your dog's supposed to be losing weight, you shouldn't give him any treats at all.

Treats are an important part of dog training — more on that in Chapter 4 — but it doesn't take very much to get the job done when it comes to rewarding your dog. Give her a tiny corner of a biscuit or a little piece of hot dog, instead of a whole biscuit or an inch-long chunk of sausage.

Understanding the Benefits of Exercise

Exercise provides immense physical and psychological benefits to dogs of all ages. Dogs who exercise regularly live longer, remain healthier, and are more active in their later years. With regular exercise, your dog will become stronger and more coordinated, and her muscles will become more powerful and ready to kick into action any time. Strong muscles stabilize the joints, slowing the progression of arthritis. Exercise strengthens the heart and the lungs as well, improving the delivery of oxygen and nutrients to tissues throughout the body. Exercise also is an excellent way to control your dog's weight; strong muscles are larger and use more calories while at rest than smaller muscles do.

Exercise can prevent a dog from developing problems such as *lick granulomas* (sores caused by repeated licking or chewing at the skin), destructive behaviors (such as chewing the corners of your new couch or digging up your tulip bulbs), restlessness, or excessive barking. In fact, exercise is so important to a dog's psyche that it's the first line of treatment for most behavioral problems. Dog behaviorists claim that lack of exercise is a significant contributing factor in more than half of all behavioral problems in dogs.

Despite all the benefits of exercise, the majority of dogs in North America don't get enough exercise. If your dog spends so much time lounging that she's starting to look like part of the furniture, it's time to get her on her feet and out of the house. Do it gradually, however. Just as you wouldn't head out the door to run a marathon without any training, you shouldn't expect your dog to be able to exercise for hours without building up to that level.

To remain fit and content, a dog should get a minimum of 15 minutes of exercise a day and should have a longer exercise period two to three times a week. Be creative with your dog's exercise (see the next section). This is a time when you and your dog can get to know each other better — make the most of it!

Mixing Up Your Dog's Exercise Routine

Like humans, dogs have a mixture of muscle fibers — some for strength and some for endurance. These fibers use energy differently and are called upon in different circumstances. Try to provide a mix of both strength-training and endurance-training exercises for your dog. Exercises such as retrieving and chasing that involve many starts, stops, and turns help build strength. Exercises such as trotting, in which the dog moves continuously for at least 20 minutes, build endurance. Dogs benefit most if you build both their strength *and* their endurance muscles. In the following sections, we offer activities that will interest you and your dog.

Inject a little variety into your playtimes. After all, too much of even a fun game gets boring. Play different kinds of games in different locales, at different times of the day, and using different treats for rewards.

Instinctive activities

Often the activities that are most fun for dogs (and their humans) are those that imitate the dog's natural drives and instincts. When your dog plays fetch, she imagines herself as a mighty hunter, chasing her prey and bringing it home to the pups. For dogs with herding instincts, such as Shelties and Collies, it's the chasing part that's fun, not the capture. They bring the ball back so they can chase it again. A pair of dogs will often exercise each other, alternating between being the chaser and the chasee. Terriers and other dogs originally bred to hunt vermin love to play games with a killing theme. Nothing feels quite as good to a terrier as chasing a stuffed toy, capturing it, and shaking it to break its neck.

You can design games around a dog's latent herding instinct by inventing chasing games. One fun game is to have your dog sit and stay in the middle of a soccer field, place yourself approximately three quarters of the way to the goal, release your dog, and start running. See which one of you gets to the goal first (but handicap yourself so your dog wins about half the time).

You can re-create vermin-catching games for your terrier. Drag a bone or a toy over the ground for 25 feet or so and then bury it in an area of the garden that you don't mind if she digs in. Watch your terrier's face beam as you take her to the beginning of the scent trail and encourage her to "find the rat."

Walking

Many people derive great pleasure from a daily walk with the dog. For some, this means an early morning stride through the neighborhood with the dew on the grass and the birds chattering in the trees. For others, it's a chance to put on the headphones, crank up the music, and forget the day's stresses. Most dogs enjoy walks because of their natural curiosity about the environment. They love to be surrounded by new sights and smells. You may find it kind of frustrating, however, to stop at each vertical object along the way so your dog can exchange pee-mail with the other dogs in the neighborhood. Try this compromise: Before going for a walk, let your dog into the yard so he can eliminate there. During the walk, let your pooch stop and communicate only on the first block. After that, give the command, "Let's go!" Make your dog get moving and not stop again until you say so.

Always carry a plastic bag and pick up after your dog (and remind your dog walker or pet sitter to do so, too). Just slip your hand in the bag, grab the dog poop, and then turn the bag inside out over your hand and tie it in a knot. Find a trash can to deposit your package in, or throw it out when you get home. Your neighbors will appreciate your thoughtfulness and you will feel good knowing that you're doing your part to keep the neighborhood dog-friendly.

Trotting

If you want to step it up a bit, take your dog for a run. (Actually your dog trots, while you keep up by any number of means. Trotting is one of the best endurance exercises for dogs.) It's not even essential for you to run alongside. You can try inline skating on a paved high school track with your dog trotting on the infield grass. Or try training your dog to trot beside your bike. Be sure to use a device such as the Springer or K-9 Cruiser to attach your dog's leash to the bicycle, leaving your hands free.

Bicycling with a loose dog is dangerous. Even on country paths, a loose dog can chase wild animals such as rabbits or deer and become lost or injured. Use an attachment that connects your dog to your bike.

Fetch

Fetch is a favorite game of many dogs. Most people are fond of this game because they can play it while standing still. You can use many different fetch objects, from a simple stick to a ball or a disc. Some balls even glow in the dark or have an internal flashing light so you can use them for a quick game of fetch when you get home from work on a dark winter night. Many dogs like to chase flying discs as well. The way the disc floats in the air and changes directions is very exciting to the canine hunter.

Be careful when playing fetch with a flying disc. Throw the disc just above the ground so your dog doesn't have to leap up to catch it. Dogs can suffer severe injuries by twisting their backs or by landing on their rear legs when trying to catch a disc.

If your dog is not much of a retriever, she may enjoy playing soccer. Use a ball that is too large and too firm for her to pick up in her teeth. Kick it around the yard, encouraging her to chase it. She will eventually get the idea and learn to push the ball around the yard herself.

Swimming

Swimming is one of the best forms of exercise for any dog. Because swimming is a non-weight-bearing activity, it strengthens the cardiovascular and muscular systems without placing stress on bones and joints. This is especially helpful for dogs with arthritis.

Many dogs naturally enjoy swimming, and most can learn if they're given encouragement when they're young. The best way to teach a pup to swim is to start by putting your boots on and walking with her in a creek. Creeks have deeper and shallower parts, and eventually, your pup will find herself swimming over a short distance without even realizing it. If your adult dog is reluctant to swim, the best way to teach her is to get wet yourself and encourage her to join you in the fun. If she is hesitant to swim over her head, use the Hansel-and-Gretel principle: Walk slowly out to deeper waters, depositing dog treats as you go (Cheerios float very well) and offering encouragement. Often, your dog's stomach will overcome her fears.

If your water-loving canine is going to swim in a pond, make sure to scout the area for broken glass, fishing lines, and other hazards first. If you find broken glass, find another place for your dog to swim, because there's likely to be more where the piece you found came from.

If you or a friend have a swimming pool and don't mind a little dog hair in the filter, letting your dog swim there is just fine.

Never let your dog swim in a pool without supervision. Every year, dogs drown in pools after becoming exhausted trying to find their way out, even when stairs are available. Plus, some breeds, such as Bulldogs, aren't built for swimming and can drown in shallow water. Be sure you know your dog's limitations.

Getting the Gear for Grooming

You can spend hundreds of dollars on grooming tools like scissors, brushes, and nail clippers. Although you don't need to spend that kind of money, investing in top-quality equipment is best: A few well-chosen pieces do the job well and last forever. In the following sections, we tell you what you need to keep your pooch sitting pretty.

Combs and brushes

For most dogs, the grooming kit starts with a comb and a brush. The ones you choose depend on your pet's coat type. If you bought your puppy or dog from a reputable breeder, you should be able to ask for equipment recommendations and grooming advice. For mixed-breeds, go with the tools best suited for the purebred your dog's coat most resembles. Choose metal combs and brushes with sturdy bristles set into a comfortable wooden handle.

Nail trimmers

Because some — okay, most — dogs don't like to have their nails trimmed, this procedure is the most often neglected piece of a regular grooming regimen. A lot of people leave it to their veterinarian or groomer, sometimes waiting until the dog must be anesthetized for another reason.

Better you should trim a little bit yourself every week than let your dog struggle with long nails. If left unattended, overgrown nails can cause lameness. And no, a daily walk isn't enough to keep them worn down.

Three kinds of nail trimmers are widely available — guillotine style, scissors style, and an electric nail grinder. The latter is the most expensive — around $50 — but is a good way to keep nails short without nicking the quick, a common problem with nail cutters. A nail grinder may be more acceptable to dogs who don't like their nails trimmed — unless they're put off by the noise and vibration.

Nail clippers are the most common, however, and whether you use the guillotine or scissors style is a matter of personal preference — both do a good, fast job. You will need a small jar of blood-stopping powder on hand when you trim nails to stop bleeding, should you cut too far. There are a couple of brands on the market; Kwik Stop is probably the best known.

Shampoos and conditioners

Remember that old saying about only washing a dog once or twice a year? Forget it! Who'd want to live with a dirty, stinky dog?

It's true that dogs don't need to wash as often as we do — because they don't sweat — but they get plenty dirty. Frequent bathing — as often as once a week — can make living with a dog manageable for many allergy sufferers, and a clean dog is just more pleasant for everyone to be around.

Maybe you've heard that frequent bathing strips the coat of its natural oils. To some extent, that's true. If you need to, you can always put back in some of what you take out, by following shampoo with a conditioner. And good nutrition has a bigger impact on a glossy coat than bathing does — so go ahead, bathe that dog.

There are oodles of shampoos — some to keep dark coats dark, others to make white coats brighter. Shampoos with every imaginable scent, shampoos for fleas, shampoos for itchiness. If your pet has a skin problem, ask your veterinarian for a recommendation. Otherwise, experiment a little to find products you like working with.

Other niceties and necessities

Depending on what kind of dog you have, you may want to add some other items to your collection of grooming supplies, including

- **Antiseptic liquid:** Nolvasan is probably the most common, a blue-tinted liquid that veterinarians use for everything from cleaning ears to disinfecting exam tables. An absolute must-have for dogs with floppy ears who swim regularly or are otherwise prone to ear infections.
- **Bath mat and spray nozzle:** A wet bathtub is slippery, and nothing makes a dog more nervous than not being able to stand square on all four paws. Some people rinse dogs by pouring dirty bath water back over them, but that defeats the purpose of bathing a dog — to get him clean — so use a nozzle. An inexpensive option is the rubber kind that fits over the bathtub tap.

- **Corn starch:** Useful for working out mats. Nonstick cooking spray can also be helpful in clearing a coat of burrs.
- **Cotton balls:** Great for cleaning the inside of the ear flap, and for wiping tear stains, skin folds, and eye gunk.
- **Old towels:** Never throw a towel away! Even the most faded, worn, and torn towel is good for drying a freshly bathed dog or wiping off muddy paws.
- **Spray bottle:** Makes brushing long-haired dogs easy, and keeps things cool for short-haired dogs while you work.
- **Tweezers:** Good for removing ear hair and ticks.

Keeping Up Appearances

Good grooming has more benefits than keeping your pet looking beautiful and smelling clean — although that's certainly one of the pleasant payoffs. Regular grooming also relaxes the dog who's used to it, and becomes a special time shared between you and your dog.

A coat free of mats, burrs, and tangles is as comfortable to your dog as clothes fresh from the wash are to you: It just makes you feel good. Properly trimmed nails make moving more comfortable, and keeping ears clean of wax and excess hair helps keep infections at bay — and eliminates another source of dreaded doggy odor. We cover each of these grooming methods in the following sections.

Brushing and combing

Have you ever had your hair in a ponytail that was just a little too tight? A mat can feel the same way to your dog, a constant pull on the skin. Try to imagine those all over your body and you have a good idea how uncomfortable an ungroomed coat can be. Even worse, an ungroomed coat can be a health hazard, as skin becomes so badly damaged that flies will lay eggs in the wounds and maggots will result. Ick!

Your dog need never know what a mat feels like if you keep him brushed and combed. You should go over him daily, clearing such things as mats and ticks from his coat and brush him out completely every week.

For short-haired breeds, run your hands over him daily, brush him weekly, and that's it. For other breeds, grooming is a little more involved. Double-coated, long-haired breeds have a downy undercoat that can mat down like a layer of felt against the skin if left untouched. To prevent this, divide the coat into small sections and brush against the grain from the skin outward, working from head to tail, section by section. In the spring and fall — the Big Shed times — you'll end up with enough of that fluffy undercoat to make a whole new dog. Keep brushing, and think of the benefits: The fur you pull out with a brush doesn't end up on the furniture, and removing the old stuff keeps your pet cooler in the summer and lets new insulation come in for the winter.

Lightly misting the part of the fur you're brushing with water from a spray bottle makes working the brush through the coat easier and helps keep the long outer coat from breaking.

Silky-coated dogs also need constant brushing to keep tangles from forming. As with the double-coated dogs, work with small sections at a time, brushing from the skin outward and then comb back into place with the grain for a glossy, finished look. Coats of this type require so much attention that having a groomer keep the dogs trimmed to a medium length is often practical.

Curly and wiry coats need to be brushed weekly, working against the grain and then with it. Curly coats need to be clipped every six weeks, wiry ones two or three times a year (but clipping every six weeks keeps your terrier looking sharper).

Learning to clip your dog yourself isn't that hard — if you don't mind a few bad hair weeks for your dog. Dog clippers are widely available in pet-supply and discount stores, and these kits contain basic instructions for keeping your pet shorn.

Every grooming session should end with a petting session, to make your dog's last impression of grooming time a pleasant one.

Giving a bath

Why is it that from the instant the first drops of water spill out of the tap, from the second you reach for the bottle of shampoo, your dog starts burrowing his way to the darkest, quietest, most hidden corner of the house? The dog who doesn't hear you when you scream, "Get off the couch!" is able to pick out the magic word when you whisper, "I think the dog needs a bath."

Like most dogs, your dog is content to live his life in dog-smell heaven, a place where water is to drink or swim in and never has soap added. Too bad. We make the rules, and dog-smell heaven is no paradise for us.

House dogs should be bathed monthly, more often still if they need it. Using a high-quality shampoo and conditioner babies the coat and replenishes some of the oils bathing removes.

Your dog should be brushed before bathing because mats and tangles, once wet, can't be removed — you need to cut them out.

Let your dog chill for a minute while you collect the bath-time basics. You don't want to be looking for shampoo while struggling with a dog determined to get out of the tub.

Dogs have a keen sense of hearing and some are upset by the sound of bath water running when they know it's for them. After the tub is full, turn off the tap and let the water sit while you prepare the dog for the big plunge. Put a pinch of cotton just inside your dog's ears and a drop of mineral oil in each eye to help keep the soap out.

Oh, and you don't have to use the bathtub. Smaller dogs can be washed in a utility tub or sink. What about outdoor bathing? Dogs have been hose-washed for generations with no ill effect, but warm water is kinder, especially for older or arthritic dogs.

As you drag the dog toward the bathroom door, don't spare words of love and encouragement. In working with dogs, a good attitude can go a long way, but a bad one can go even farther. If your dog knows how much you hate bath time, how can he get a positive — or at least tolerable — opinion of the process? Keep your attitude high and don't let up on the praise.

Start shampooing by working a complete ring of lather around the neck, cutting off the fleas' escape route to the ears. Work forward and back from there, and don't forget to work some lather between your dog's toes — another favorite get-away for fleas. Empty the anal sacs and suds the area thoroughly. Rinse thoroughly, and repeat the entire process if need be before conditioning. Then lift your dog out and put a towel over him loosely while he shakes. Your dog can get more water off by shaking than you can by toweling, so let him have at it, and then finish the job by rubbing him dry when he's done.

Trimming toenails

Many dog owners avoid trimming toenails. Toenail trims can turn into a hard-fought war with bloody casualties on both sides. Because of that, many people leave the task of trimming nails to their groomer or veterinarian — but unless you're seeing these professionals a lot more than most people, your pet's nails aren't being trimmed often enough. Long nails can make walking uncomfortable and can even cause lameness, which is why trimming nails short — they should be just off the ground when your pet is standing — and then trimming them just a pinch every week is a better way to go.

The problem with nails is that each has a blood vessel inside. The trick is to trim to just beyond the end of this vein; if you nick it, the nail will bleed, and your dog will yelp. Everyone hits this vein on occasion, even veterinarians, which is why you should be sure to have blood-stopping powder on hand, such as Kwik Stop, before you start trimming. If your dog has light-colored toenails, the blood vessel is the pink area.

Black nails are harder to figure out, but you should be able to see the vein by shining a flashlight behind the nail. If you can't tell, just clip back a little at a time. If you draw blood, take a pinch of the powder and press it against the exposed bottom of the nail for a few seconds to stop the bleeding.

If your dog's resistant to having her nails trimmed, work up to the task slowly by touching her feet, then her toes, then the nails, all while praising her for holding still. When she is used to having her feet handled, put the trimmer against the nail and praise more still. Then trim a little off, and so on. Praise and more praise! The process can take several weeks, working at it every night, but if you're patient, consistent, and persistent, you'll get there.

Another way around the Toe-Trim Wrestlerama is to try the peanut butter trick. Put a big dollop of peanut butter on the door of your refrigerator at your pup's nose level. While your dog is licking up the PB, trim his nails.

Special care for special ears

No matter what kind of dog you have, but especially if yours is of a floppy-eared variety, an important part of your weekly grooming routine should be to lift your dog's ear flaps and take a big sniff.

What are you checking for? It's hard to describe, but chances are you'll know it when you sniff it. Dogs with yeast or bacterial infections in their ears have a smell you can easily diagnose with a good sniff. All the crud in the ear will be a dead giveaway, too.

Ear infections can be very difficult to eradicate. You'll need your veterinarian's help, and you'll need plenty of patience.

If your dog's ears look and smell fine, you can help to keep them that way by regular grooming. All dogs can benefit from having the insides of their ear flaps cleaned with some rubbing alcohol or Nolvasan solution (available from your vet) on a cotton ball. Nolvasan, or a similar antiseptic product, can also be used to clear the ear canal. Fill your dog's ear with the solution, and then massage the base of the ear to loosen dirt and debris. Let your dog have a good shake, and dab the ear and inner flap with a cotton ball to clean up the mess. Then do the same for the other ear.

Check your dog's ears weekly, and clean them out — well — monthly. If your dog's a swimmer, it wouldn't hurt to clean them out after every trip to the water — dogs get swimmer's ear, too!

If your dog's ear is full of wax and debris, is tender to the touch, or is smelly, you need to take him to your veterinarian for treatment.

Don't take ear care lightly, and definitely don't ignore it altogether. Ear infections can be a source of considerable discomfort for your dog.

Chapter 6

Keeping Your Dog Healthy

In This Chapter

- Knowing the importance of vaccinating and neutering your dog
- Keeping fleas, ticks, and worms at bay
- Putting together a first-aid kit
- Treating common illnesses and injuries

Just a few decades ago, in order to make it to adulthood, puppies had to avoid or successfully battle a variety of deadly diseases. And fleas were a part of every dog's life — along with the scratching, infections, and allergies that accompany those irritating insects. But scientists and veterinarians have developed vaccines that prevent canine infectious diseases to keep dogs healthy and prolong their lives.

And just like humans, dogs can get sick or injured. Although you can take some safety precautions to help your dog avoid these pitfalls, you can't guarantee that she'll never run into trouble. And that's where knowing first aid comes in handy.

In this chapter, I tell you everything you need to know to prevent disease from hitting your dog and how to care for your dog when she's injured or ill. Knowing what to do to keep your dog healthy will give your dog a better chance of living a long and healthy life, which means more time for you to play fetch, teach her tricks, run with her, let her lick your face. . . .

Vaccinating Your Dog

Today vaccinations are such a routine part of veterinary visits that most dog owners aren't aware of what a benefit they have been to dogs' health. Just a few decades ago, thousands of dogs died or were permanently disabled every year by the dreaded distemper virus, which usually attacks puppies under 1 year of age. Now we rarely hear of a dog with distemper, except in unvaccinated populations.

In 1978, canine parvovirus first appeared and began killing thousands of puppies — often entire litters — throughout the world. Veterinary scientists worked feverishly to develop a vaccine against this virus, and within a few short years, most dogs were protected by a simple vaccination.

Puppies should get their first set of vaccinations at 6 to 8 weeks of age. They also need two more sets of vaccinations spaced three to four weeks apart before they are fully immunized.

Talk to your veterinarian about setting up a vaccination schedule. The vaccinations you select for your dog will depend on her age, where you live, and the chances of your dog being exposed to infected dogs or wildlife.

Table 6-1 lists the diseases you can vaccinate against, along with the symptoms they result in when a dog has the disease.

Table 6-1 Diseases You Can Vaccinate Against and Their Symptoms

Disease	*Symptoms*
Rabies	Salivation, aggression, paralysis
Distemper	Diarrhea, pneumonia, tremors
Parvovirus	Bloody diarrhea, dehydration
Infectious Canine Hepatitis	Diarrhea, pneumonia
Coronavirus	Diarrhea
Kennel cough	Cough, pneumonia
Lyme disease	Lameness, arthritis
Leptospirosis	Bloody urine, diarrhea, vomiting

Neutering Your Dog

The only way to be sure your dog doesn't produce puppies is to get your female dog spayed or your male dog castrated.

Intact male dogs and bitches in heat have an uncanny way of finding each other, and a breeding can occur in a snap.

Spaying involves the removal of both the uterus and the ovaries. *Castration* refers to the removal of a male dog's testicles. The term *neutering* is a general term to describe either spaying or castration (but you may hear the terms neutering and castrating used to mean the same thing).

In addition to preventing unwanted puppies, neutering your dog has many benefits:

- Female dogs who are spayed prior to their first heat cycle (which usually occurs between 6 and 9 months of age) have a significantly reduced chance of developing mammary (breast) cancer compared to dogs who have had even one heat cycle.
- Spayed females can't develop *pyometra,* an infection of the uterus that can be quite severe and can even result in death.
- Spayed females tend to have more even temperaments and don't go through the hormone-induced mood swings that intact bitches sometimes have.
- Neutered dogs often are better behaved than their intact counterparts. Not only are they less likely to roam (visiting neighborhood females is a major reason for roaming), they are also less likely to mark their territory by urinating in the house. In addition, neutered male dogs are much less likely to be aggressive toward other male dogs.
- Neutering prevents the development of prostate problems and testicular cancer.

Getting Rid of Fleas, Ticks, and Worms

An important part of prevention is keeping your dog free of all the nasty creatures who like to use her body as their home or feeding ground. In the following sections, we let you know how to prevent fleas, ticks, and worms from bothering your dog — and what to do if they already have.

Making fleas flee

Fleas are the quintessential reproductive success story. A pair of fleas in your home can grow into a major infestation within a few weeks, and every one of those fleas is interested in just one thing: food in the form of blood. And to make matters worse, these insect vampires do not care where the blood comes from — your dog, your cat, or you — and the more blood they get, the more they reproduce. If your cute little canine brings a male and a female flea home, these two fleas can populate your home with 250,000 descendants within one month!

Fleas love moist, humid weather, making the southeastern United States the flea capital of North America. For dog lovers in warm climates, flea control requires constant vigilance. Fleas don't survive freezing temperatures, however, so in colder climes, the winter weather naturally decreases the flea population every year. In these areas, fleas are most abundant during the fall, when temperatures are dropping and fleas are moving indoors to ride out the winter months.

You may first become aware that your dog has fleas when you see her strenuously scratching her ears and neck. She also may suddenly turn and bite vigorously at her rear legs or rear end. If you see this kind of behavior, you need to check for fleas on your furry friend.

With your dog lying down, separate the hairs around the base of her tail (a favorite flea hangout), along the backs of her legs, on her stomach, and around her neck and ears. If you see tiny black or brown irregular pieces of dirt, it may be flea dirt, which consists of dried blood and flea excrement. If you want to know whether it's flea dirt or regular old yard dirt, smear some on a damp paper towel. If the smear is reddish brown, like dried blood, you can be fairly certain it has come from fleas.

An easy way to detect fleas or flea dirt is to have your dog lie on a clean white sheet while you brush her or blow her hair with a dryer. This may stir up a few fleas, making them jump off the dog and onto the sheet, where you can easily see them (they are dark brown, less than ⅛-inch long, and shaped like a flat oval). Even if you don't see the fleas themselves, you can easily spot flea dirt on the white sheet.

If you see even one flea on your dog, you can be certain there are at least a hundred more in one form or another (eggs, larvae, or adults) on your dog, in the carpet, and wherever your dog sleeps. It's time to go into flea attack mode! Here are the steps to completely free your dog and your environment of these freeloaders:

1. **Bathe your dog carefully.**

   Make sure to cover the entire dog with lather from the shampoo, keeping the shampoo on the dog for several minutes, which can suffocate fleas on the dog.

2. **Gather up your dog's bedding (and your own bed linens if your dog shares your bed) and throw them in the washing machine.**

3. **Vacuum all areas of the house to which your dog has access.**

   Place the vacuum bag in a plastic bag and tape it securely shut before disposing of it outside. Otherwise, the little critters will hop out and reinfest your house.

If you use this multi-pronged attack immediately upon seeing the first flea, you stand a reasonable chance of banishing the bloodthirsty critters from your house. But it would, of course, be better if your dog never brought one of the sneaky critters home.

Here are a few tips to prevent fleas from coming to visit in the first place:

- Use a once-a-month topical or oral flea treatment (the best known brands are Advantage, Frontline, and Program) that kills fleas on your dog within hours. These products are not pesticides; they are insect growth regulators, which prevent the development and growth of fleas.
- Sprinkle diatomaceous earth or boric acid on the floor. These products dehydrate fleas and flea larvae, and they don't contain any chemicals that can harm pets or children.
- Vacuum frequently to help control the flea population in the carpet. Place the vacuum bag in a plastic bag (so fleas can't escape), and throw it away.
- Wash your dog's bedding weekly to reduce the chances of a flea family setting up shop there.

Getting ticked off at ticks

Ticks are bad news: They transmit several diseases that can cause severe illness and even death in both dogs and humans.

Huge numbers of tick eggs hatch each spring, and the young ticks climb onto grasses and other vegetation. Their sticky shells help them to cling to passing animals, including your adventurous canine. They quickly climb down the hair, attach to the skin, and begin to suck blood, only dropping off hours or days later when they are engorged. In the meantime, any microorganisms that were hitching a ride inside this insect traveler are transmitted to your dog through the tick's mouth.

Keeping your dog as free of ticks as possible is always the safest bet — not only for your dog, but for you as well. Here are some tick-prevention tips:

- During the tick season (April through September), limit your dog's exposure to known tick-infested areas. Ticks often hide in tall grasses and dense vegetation.
- Use a tick preventive during the spring and summer months. Several products on the market kill both fleas and ticks (and why not knock out both at the same time?). You can apply these products monthly to the skin at the back of your dog's neck. Ask your veterinarian to recommend the most effective product for your dog.
- Examine your dog for ticks daily during tick season. If you suspect she has been romping in a tick-infested area, examine her for ticks immediately. Be sure to check inside and behind her ears and around her eyes, all favorite tick hiding places.
- Carefully remove all ticks and dispose of them in a sealed plastic bag. Be sure to remove the entire tick from your dog's body.

To remove a tick, use a pair of tweezers to grasp the head of the tick where it attaches to the skin. (Wear gloves if you plan to use your fingers to remove the tick.) Apply gentle traction. In about 20 to 30 seconds, the tick's mouth will release its grasp on the dog's skin and the tick will come away cleanly. Dab some disinfectant on the bitten area. If you yank the tick away from your dog too quickly, you'll leave part of the tick's mouth behind, which can cause an infection. Kill the tick by placing it in alcohol. Save the dead tick in a resealable plastic bag, labeled with the date on which the tick was found. This may sound weird, but if your dog becomes ill, you may need to identify the species of tick that bit her.

If your dog becomes ill and you recently found a tick on her, immediately seek veterinary attention. Most tick-borne diseases can be treated successfully if a diagnosis is made immediately and appropriate treatment initiated. If the tick-borne organisms are allowed to gain a foothold, however, these bad bugs can cause serious illness or death.

Whipping worms for good

Several kinds of worms can live in your dog's intestines and cause abdominal pain, diarrhea, or anemia. Roundworms are predominantly a puppy problem. Puppies can be infected by their mothers even before they are born. These worms can be so numerous that they cause intestinal blockage. They can also work their way up into the dog's stomach and cause vomiting. All puppies should be treated for roundworms as a part of their regular veterinary checkup.

Whipworms and hookworms can infest dogs of all ages. A dog becomes infected when she eats egg-laden feces from an infected dog. These worms attach to the wall of the intestine and gnaw away. A large infestation can cause significant blood loss, which can result in anemia.

Bring a fecal sample from your dog to each annual checkup, at least until your dog is 3 or 4 years old. A veterinary technician will check for worm eggs while the veterinarian examines your dog. If your pooch has parasites, a pill can usually put her right.

Assembling a Canine First-Aid Kit

Before your dog gets sick or you're faced with a canine emergency, assemble a first-aid kit for your dog. Administering first aid is very difficult — if not impossible — without a few essential supplies. Always keep the kit in the same place so you can get your hands on it right away in an emergency.

Getting the container ready

Find a water-resistant container that's large enough to carry everything without being cumbersome. Fishing tackle boxes work well because they have trays with dividers to keep things organized.

Put a large red cross and the words "first-aid kit" on each side of the container. Someone may need to locate and use it in an emergency, and labeling the kit clearly can be a big help.

To the inside of the lid, tape a piece of paper with the following information in clear letters:

- The breed, name, and date of birth of your dog.
- Any medical conditions your dog has and any medication she takes regularly.
- The name, address, and telephone number of your veterinarian.
- Contact information for the National Animal Poison Control Center. You can reach them at 888-426-4435 24 hours a day, 365 days a year to inquire about the toxic potential of various household products and plants your dog may have found tasty. For a fee, you also can get advice about emergency care for a dog who has gotten into a toxin.
- A list of the contents of your first-aid kit. For each of the drugs in the kit, you should also have a note indicating the appropriate dose for your dog. That way you won't have to do any calculations in your head in a time of crisis. When preparing the kit, be sure to check the doses with your veterinarian.

Stocking the first-aid kit

Following is a list of the components of an all-purpose first-aid kit and a brief description of what each item is used for. You can find most of these items at your local pharmacy; the rest you can purchase from your veterinarian or from a dog supply catalog.

- **ACE brand elastic bandage.** You can use this bandage to hold an ice pack to a dog's leg, to wrap a sprain temporarily until you can get veterinary assistance, or to secure an injured dog to a makeshift stretcher.

- **Adhesive tape.** Use tape to secure bandages and splints.
- **Alcohol swabs.** Look for individually packaged swabs, which you can use to sterilize instruments or small areas of skin.
- **Aspirin (enteric coated).** Give 5 milligrams per pound every 12 hours to temporarily relieve pain. Many dogs vomit after taking regular aspirin, so be sure to get the enteric-coated variety.

  Never substitute ibuprofen or acetaminophen for aspirin. Both of these substances can be very toxic to dogs.
- **Athlete's foot powder.** Shake a little powder into an infected ear after cleaning it. If your dog is susceptible to ear infections, you can also shake a little powder into her ears once a week and after swimming, to prevent infection.
- **Bacitracin or Neosporin.** Apply this or another antibiotic ointment to wounds that may be dirty and are likely to become infected.

  Never use these ointments in the eye. Special antibacterial formulations are used for the eyes, and these should be used only with your veterinarian's recommendation.
- **Benadryl.** You can use Benadryl for insect bites or stings. Give your dog 1 to 2 milligrams per pound, every 8 hours.
- **Blunt-ended scissors.** Use these for cutting bandages and tape and for trimming the hair around a wound.
- **Cohesive bandage.** Use this stretchy wrap to cover and secure gauze bandages. It clings to itself so you don't need adhesive tape.
- **Cold pack.** Use a cold pack to prevent or reduce swelling after a sprain or strain or to treat burns. Buy the kind that becomes cold when you fold the pack in half.
- **Cotton squares.** You can use these to clean and protect wounds. They're better for cleaning wounds than cotton balls because they don't shed fibers when you wipe them over sticky areas such as where blood is drying.
- **First-aid instructions.** Photocopy the pages of this chapter that discuss first-aid treatments and store it in your first-aid kit. That way you will have written instructions always available in an emergency.

- **Gauze bandage roll.** You can use these to bandage wounds and to hold splints in place. Cut off a length of bandage and fold it up to cover a wound, or wrap the bandage around the leg to keep a cold pack in place or to secure a splint to the leg.
- **Gloves (latex).** Any time you need to keep your hands protected or clean, wear a pair of latex gloves.
- **Green Soap or Hibitane.** You can use any gentle liquid antibacterial soap used for cleaning skin and wounds.
- **Hydrogen peroxide.** Give your dog 1 to 3 teaspoons of hydrogen peroxide every 10 minutes to induce vomiting. Don't give more than three doses 10 minutes apart. Do not use it to clean wounds.
- **Muzzle.** You can use a length of gauze bandage, a belt, or a soft rope to make an emergency muzzle for your dog. Even if your dog has never showed signs of aggression before, if she is in pain or frightened, she may snap at you, so be sure to muzzle her — for your safety and hers.
- **NuSkin liquid bandage.** Use this to close a small, clean, recent wound.
- **Penlight flashlight.** Use a flashlight to look down your dog's ears or throat — anywhere you need extra light. You can also use it to check whether a dog's eyes respond to light in case of an injury to the head.
- **Pepto-Bismol liquid.** Give 1 teaspoon per 25 pounds every 6 hours to relive diarrhea and vomiting.
- **Plastic bags (resealable).** These are handy for temporarily packaging items that are leaking, protecting open packages from drying, or collecting specimens such as fecal samples.
- **Safety pins.** You can use safety pins to fasten bandages together if you don't have tape.
- **Sterile saline solution.** Use this to rinse out the eyes or to clean wounds.
- **Styptic powder.** Use this to stop small areas of bleeding, such as when you accidentally clip your dog's nails too close.
- **Syringe.** Use a syringe to flush your dog's eye with saline or to administer peroxide to induce vomiting.

- **Thermometer (rectal).** Use a thermometer made for dogs. A dog's normal body temperature is between 100.5 and 102.8 degrees.
- **Tweezers (flat-ended).** You can use these to remove foreign objects, such as ticks, thorns, and foxtails, from your dog's skin.

Giving First-Aid Treatment

When you're sure that an injured dog is breathing and has a pulse, you can start attending to her injuries. In the following sections, I cover some common injuries and problems requiring first aid.

Knowing these first aid techniques should help you in an emergency. But remember, this is first aid — basic techniques to help you aid your dog before you can get veterinary assistance. First aid is not a substitute for the care and expertise of a veterinarian.

Allergic reactions

In addition to normal allergic reactions (like itching and sneezing), some dogs may experience more severe symptoms, including the following:

- **Hives or swelling of the muzzle.** Some dogs respond to an allergen with swelling of the face or bumps that appear over a large part of the trunk. You may also see the dog biting or licking at herself, or she may have red, weeping eyes. Apply a cold pack to the swollen area if it is small. If the swelling continues or there is swelling over a large area, administer Benadryl (at 1 to 2 milligrams per pound) and contact your veterinarian. Check your dog's respiration periodically, because there may also be swelling of the throat, which can impair her breathing.
- **Shock.** Signs of shock include weak or rapid pulse, shallow breathing, gray, purple, or pale gums, glazed eyes, weakness, or collapse. Lay the dog on her side and cover her with a blanket. Administer CPR if necessary. Transport the dog to a veterinarian as soon as possible.

Bleeding

To stop bleeding, apply pressure to the wound with a piece of gauze or cloth for several minutes. Even if the gauze is soaked with blood, don't lift it to see if the bleeding has stopped because the gauze helps clot the blood. Just add more gauze. Depending on the area of the body and the size of the wound, it may take 10 to 15 minutes for bleeding to stop.

If ice is available, place it around the area of the wound to slow blood flow. Once the bleeding has stopped, you can bandage the wound (see the "Wounds" section later in this chapter) and arrange to get the dog to a veterinarian for assessment.

Never use a tourniquet to stop bleeding because it can cut off necessary circulation to the area.

Broken bones

When your dog has a fracture, the goal is to stabilize the dog until she can be examined and treated by a veterinarian. A broken bone will be very painful in the area of the break. Fractures are sometimes obvious, such as when the leg is lying in an abnormal position or when a piece of bone is poking through the skin. But sometimes a fracture may be present when the leg looks only swollen. If you try to move the bones, you may feel a grinding under your fingers caused by the two broken ends of the bone rubbing against each other.

If veterinary care is available, do not apply a splint. Carefully place the dog on a firm, level surface and take her to the clinic. If you are far from veterinary help, the leg should carefully be splinted before your dog is moved. The best splint is something rigid but padded such as a board wrapped in a towel. The splint should be placed against the dog's limb, avoiding movement of the bones as much as possible. The leg and joints above and below the break should be taped or wrapped to the splint. Transport the dog to a veterinary clinic as soon as possible.

Burns

Dogs are most often burned when hot or strong acids or cleaning solutions are spilled on them. Burns may also be caused when a dog gets too close to a candle, a stove, or a fire. Some dogs can even get a blistering sunburn, especially on the first sunny day after the winter.

Burns are classified by degrees, depending on their severity:

- **First degree:** In a first-degree burn, the hair is singed and the skin may be reddened.
- **Second degree:** In a second-degree burn the hair is burned off and the skin is red and blistered.
- **Third degree:** In a third degree burn, the skin is black, brown, or white. If the third-degree burn is extensive, the dog may go into shock.

If the burn was caused by a caustic liquid, wipe or rinse it off before treating it. For all burns, here are treatment suggestions:

- **Minor burns (first and second degree):** If the burn occurred within the last hour, apply a cold pack for 20 to 30 minutes and then treat the burn as a superficial wound (see "Wounds" later in this chapter).
- **Severe burns (third degree):** If your dog permits, apply a cold pack or a cold, wet cloth to the area, cover gently with gauze, and take her to the veterinarian as soon as possible.

  Never apply ointments or butter to severe burns, and never touch the skin or rub anything on it.

Cold exposure

Hypothermia is a lowering of the dog's body temperature caused by cold exposure. Dogs don't suffer from hypothermia very often because they carry their fur coats with them everywhere they go. However, if a dog is wet or if she has a very thin coat, she may get cold quite easily. The first response that a dog has when she's cold is to shiver. Later, the dog may act lethargic and become unresponsive.

If you recognize that your dog has hypothermia, do the following:

- Move the dog to a warm environment and cover her with a blanket.
- Rub her body (not her legs) gently to increase circulation.

- If she's wet, dry her with towels or a blow dryer on medium heat.
- Take your dog's temperature to monitor her recovery.
- Offer warm sugar water if the dog is conscious.

Do not apply sources of heat, such as heating pads or hot water bottles, directly to your dog's skin.

If the dog begins to lick her paws or appears uncomfortable, she may have frostbite. Restrain the dog and place warm compresses on the affected area.

Diarrhea

If you have a dog long enough, you'll have to deal with diarrhea eventually. Diarrhea can be caused by a dog's propensity to eat garbage or rotten animals, by a viral or bacterial infection, or sometimes just by stress.

If your dog has diarrhea, withhold food for 24 hours in adults or 12 hours in puppies (under 6 months). Instead of water, offer the dog ice cubes, so that she takes in the water slowly. Administer Pepto-Bismol (1 teaspoon per 25 pounds every six hours) to help calm an upset stomach and stop diarrhea. For the next 72 hours, feed the dog a bland diet (75 percent rice, 25 percent low-fat protein such as skinless chicken) in small but gradually increasing amounts. Then shift to the dog's regular diet over the next two days.

If your dog has bloody diarrhea, is depressed and dull, or continues to have diarrhea for 24 hours while you are withholding food, she should be examined by a veterinarian.

Ear infections

Chronic ear infections are extremely uncomfortable to dogs and can affect hearing and balance. If your dog has ever had an ear infection, check her ears weekly and keep them clean — this is the best way to prevent infections and to recognize them quickly when they do occur.

To clean the ears, moisten a cotton square with alcohol or hydrogen peroxide and clean the outer ear, making sure to clean around all the bumps inside the ear and down into the ear canal. Don't go farther into the canal than you can see — you don't want to risk breaking the eardrum. Shake athlete's foot powder into the ear — it has drying properties and acts as an antifungal. If your dog has hair inside her ear canal, pluck it regularly to help with air circulation.

Eyes

The eyes are very delicate and easily injured, especially in dogs who love to play in the great outdoors.

Dogs who run through fields may get dust or grasses in their eyes. The best solution is to wash the eye with sterile saline. Hold your dog's eye open and gently pour the saline over the surface of the eye. Using a penlight flashlight, examine the insides of the lids to be sure you removed the offending particles. If repeated flushing doesn't help, get your dog to a veterinarian.

If a foreign body is penetrating the eye or the skin near the eye, do not touch it. Stop the dog from pawing at the eye by taping her hind legs together or by having her wear an Elizabethan collar (a wide plastic or cardboard cone-shaped collar that prevents the dog from being able to scratch her head). You can make a temporary Elizabethan collar by cutting a head-sized hole into the bottom of a bucket and placing the bucket over the dog's head, fastening the bucket to the dog's collar. Then get your dog to a veterinarian immediately.

Heatstroke

The temperature doesn't have to be very high for a dog to suffer heatstroke. A dog suffering from heatstroke will pant heavily and salivate excessively. Her eyes may be glazed and she will stagger or act listless. The dog's pulse will be rapid and weak.

If you suspect your dog is suffering from heatstroke, you must act quickly. Move the dog to a cool area indoors or at least to the shade. Submerge her in cool water (not ice water), and apply cold compresses to her head. Take her temperature to monitor her body's cooling. Keep her wet until her temperature reaches 103 degrees, and then remove her from the water and dry her off. Encourage but do not force her to drink water. Get her to the veterinarian as soon as possible.

More dogs die of heatstroke in cars than any other way. Even on a mild day, the temperature in a car in the sun can rise to over 100 degrees in a matter of minutes. Every year, thousands of dogs die of heatstroke after being left in cars for "just a minute." Never leave your dog in the car in the summer, even with the windows down. And never leave your dog in a yard without shade in the summer.

Hot spots

Hot spots are localized areas of skin infection that are usually round, red, and warm to the touch. They can start very quickly and can grow to several inches in diameter in a matter of a day or two. The infection is exacerbated by the dog's scratching or chewing.

The first thing to do if you identify a hot spot is to clip the hair away from the area, if possible. This is the best way to prevent the infection from spreading. Once or twice a day, wash the area thoroughly with liquid soap and apply an astringent. The best astringent is tea (green or black). Wet a tea bag and apply it to the area. Keep applying the astringent several times a day until the area is dry and covered with a scab — usually 24 to 36 hours. After the area is scabbed, let it heal, but watch it carefully in case the infection begins to spread again. Keep the dog from scratching or biting at the area while it is healing; you may need to use an Elizabethan collar (see the "Eyes" section earlier in this chapter for more information). If you cannot get the hot spot under control in 36 hours, see your veterinarian, who may prescribe oral antibiotics and/or anti-inflammatory agents to treat it.

Insect bites

Usually an insect bite will appear as an area of swelling. If the bite is from a bee or a wasp, remove the stinger. If it is from a tick that is still attached, use tweezers to grasp the tick as close to the skin as possible and pull gently until it lets go (see the "Getting Rid of Fleas, Ticks, and Worms" section earlier in this chapter for more information on removing ticks). Apply a cold pack if the swelling is severe.

Sprains and strains

A sprain is a torn ligament and a strain is torn tendon, but the results of both injuries are the same — swelling and inflammation in the area of damage. The key to treating these injuries is to get ice onto the affected area immediately. Apply the ice for 20 minutes, then remove the ice for 20 minutes, and then apply ice again for 20 minutes. The ice will help to reduce the swelling and keep further damage to a minimum.

Try bandaging the ice onto the affected area if your dog doesn't want to let you hold the ice on her body for that long.

Take your dog to a veterinarian if you suspect a fracture or if your dog doesn't bear some weight on the leg within an hour or two. The dog should rest for at least 48 hours after the injury — no running or playing, just short walks on a leash to go potty. If the dog is still limping after 48 hours, she should be seen by a veterinarian.

Wounds

In their inimitable love of life, dogs can get themselves into some pretty fixes. They may run into tree branches or rub against sharp objects. They may even get in an occasional fight and end up a little worse for the wear. So knowing what to do for your walking wounded canine is important.

Wounds fall into two main categories: shallow and deep. Shallow wounds involve just the skin; deep wounds penetrate to the muscles and other tissues below the skin.

To treat a shallow wound:

1. **Wash your hands thoroughly.**
2. **Use cotton squares and mild antibacterial liquid soap to clean the wound thoroughly.**
3. **Rinse the wound with sterile saline solution.**

4. **Apply antibacterial ointment to the wound.**
5. **Cover the wound with gauze, wrap it with a bandage, and cover it with cohesive bandage (but not so tight that you cut off circulation).**
6. **Periodically feel your dog's toes.**

   If they become swollen or cool to the touch, remove the bandage and reapply it after the swelling has diminished.

If the wound is small and clean, you can use NuSkin to glue the ends of the wound together. It works just like sutures.

To treat a deep wound:

1. **Stop the bleeding by applying pressure.**
2. **When the bleeding has stopped, bandage the wound and seek immediate veterinary treatment.**

Cuts that may require sutures should be examined by a veterinarian immediately. If a cut is more than about six hours old, it should not be sutured closed because it almost certainly is contaminated with bacteria from the environment. Suturing the wound closed would just trap the bacteria within the wound, resulting in infection and increased scarring. An older cut should be thoroughly cleaned and allowed to heal gradually as an open wound. If the wound is large, it may be partially sutured and a drain left in to help the infection escape.

Chapter 7

Ten Tips for Traveling with Your Dog

In This Chapter

- Making sure your companion is well mannered
- Knowing what to pack for your pooch
- Traveling by car and air
- Choosing a dog-friendly vacation
- Finding care for the stay-at-home pet

Traveling with dogs is not new, of course. The unique combination of companionship and protection that dogs offer has made them welcome on trips from the very beginning of our centuries-old partnership with them.

Recreational travel for dogs, however, has never been more popular. Dogs can be seen at the roughest campsites and the swankiest hotels. No matter what your destination, the tips in this chapter can help you make travel safe and fun for you and your four-legged friend.

Travel Manners Are a Must

The minimum requirement for canine travelers is that they be able to behave themselves on-leash in some very exciting circumstances — around strange people, strange dogs, and strange scenery, sounds, and smells. If you plan to let your dog off-leash, you'd better be sure that she'll come when called and leave something — like a dead fish on the beach — alone when you ask her to. She should also be trained to stop barking on command.

"Sit"? "Down"? "Stay"? Are these foreign concepts to your dog? All you need to know to make your dog a well-mannered companion is in Chapter 4.

Pack a Doggie Suitcase

You can really go crazy packing things to ensure your dog's safety and comfort. Here are the basics of what little Lucy will need:

- **A sturdy collar with a license and an up-to-date ID tag.** The tag should include your cellphone number. Ideally, your pet should also be carrying an imbedded microchip for unshakable, permanent ID.
- **A 6-foot leash.** A longer leash is handy, too, especially a reel-type leash, which is great for giving your dog a little room to stretch her legs in areas such as rest stops.
- **Two bowls, one for food, one for water.** Bowls that either collapse for easy storage or don't spill are perfect for travel.
- **Food.** If your dog's on a widely available brand of food, pack enough to get you started and pick up the rest on the road, if you're going to an area with a market or pet-supplies store. Prescription food or anything out of the ordinary you'll have to bring along enough for the trip. If your pet eats canned food, you need a spoon or fork, and a can opener unless your pup's brand comes in pop-tops.
- **Treats!**
- **A comb, brush, and tweezers.** These come in handy for pulling ticks, especially on back-country trips.
- **Basic first-aid supplies.** Handy items include scissors, gauze, tape, and Pepto-Bismol for diarrhea. See Chapter 6 for more on first-aid kits.
- **Any regular medication your pet takes.**
- **Cloth towels and paper towels.** You'll want cloth towels for drying off wet, dirty dogs; you'll use the paper towels for cleaning up more things than you can imagine.
- **Plastic bags.** These are a must-bring for poop pick-ups.
- **A couple of your pup's favorite toys!**

Bring Emergency Papers

As with anything else, the key for traveling with a dog is, prepare for the worst, hope for the best. Carry some ready-made LOST DOG! fliers with your dog's picture on them and a place to write a phone number with a big marker. Don't forget your pet's health records, including microchip number, and especially proof of rabies vaccination. The latter is absolutely imperative should the unthinkable happen: Your dog bites someone or tangles with a rabid creature in the wild.

Make Car Rides Safer

As with all other training, ending up with a good car rider starts with molding correct behavior when your dog is a puppy. No matter how cute or how small, do not allow your pup to ride in your lap, and don't make a fuss over him while you're driving.

Traveling with your dog in a crate is often easier and definitely safer. Depending on the size of your dog and the size and shape of your car, a crate may not be feasible. Crates should always be considered, though, especially for those dogs who are so active they distract the driver. Collapsible crates are available for easy storage in the trunk when not in use.

Another safety tool is a doggie seat belt, which fits into a standard seat-belt buckle and then attaches to a harness on the dog.

Help Your Dog Keep Her Cool

Just about everyone understands that dogs shouldn't be left inside a car on a hot day, but few realize the danger is just as great on a warm one. It's a horrible way to die.

A car functions similarly to a greenhouse, and heat can build up to lethal levels in minutes, even on a pleasant day in the 70s or low 80s. Even with the windows rolled down, a dog can show signs of heat stress — heavy panting, glazed eyes, rapid pulse, dizziness or vomiting, or a deep red or purple tongue — in the time it takes you to get a six-pack through the 12 Items or Less line. Brain damage and death can follow within minutes.

An overheated dog needs prompt veterinary attention to have a chance at survival. Don't delay! Better yet: Don't risk your dog's life by leaving him in the car.

Travel by Air

If you and your dog don't travel by car in the United States, air is your only other option. The major bus lines and Amtrak don't allow any animals except those serving the disabled.

Airline travel is relatively safe for most dogs, and it will be for yours if you play by the rules, plan carefully, and are prepared to be a little pushy on your pet's behalf.

Animals move through the airline system in two ways: as cargo or as accompanied baggage. Either way, almost all of these animals will travel in a pressurized cargo hold beneath the passenger compartment. Although the accommodations aren't any nicer, it's better for your pet if he is traveling as your "baggage," so you can ask about him in person.

Some airlines allow small dogs in the cabin, if their carriers can fit in the space beneath the seat. This is by far the best way that your dog can fly, because he never leaves your care during the course of the trip. Not all airlines allow dogs to travel in the cabin, however, and others put a limit on the number of dogs in the cabin, so make your arrangements far in advance. The only larger dogs allowed in the cabin are service dogs traveling with a disabled person.

Keep the following points in mind when making travel arrangements for your dog:

- **Talk to the airline.** Some carriers — especially the no-frills companies — don't take animals at all. Even those that do, have limits to the number of animals on a flight because a set amount of air is available in the sealed cargo holds. You also need to know where and when your dog has to be presented, and what papers — health certificate, and so on — you need to bring.
- **Be sure that your dog is in good health.**
- **Be sure that your dog is traveling in a proper carrier that has contact phone numbers at both ends of the journey.**

The crate should be just big enough for your dog to stand up and turn around in. (See Chapter 2 for more on crates.)

- **Don't ship your pet when the weather is bad or when air traffic is heaviest.** Avoid peak travel days such as around the Christmas holidays, and be sure to choose flights that are on the ground when the temperature is neither too hot nor too cold, not only at the departure airport but also at the connecting and arriving airports. In summer, a night flight is likely better, while the reverse is true in the winter.
- **Fly with your dog whenever possible.** Keeping on top of things is easier when you're on the same flight.
- **Choose a direct flight.** If that's not possible, try for a route with a short layover.
- **Be assertive.** Your dog's life relies on the attentiveness of airline personnel. Most of these employees are excellent and caring, but mistakes do happen. You should be prepared to pester airline personnel to confirm your dog has been loaded and has made the same connections you have.

Find Dog-Friendly Quarters

Just as vacations with children are different from adults-only trips, traveling with your dog works out better if you plan the journey with an eye to finding places where dogs are not only welcome but are also able to enjoy the surroundings.

When looking for lodging that accepts your four-footed friend, call ahead. Even the most dog-friendly places may have only a couple of rooms available for dog lovers, and if these are in popular resorts areas, they can be booked months in advance for prime vacation weekends.

Choose a Doggie Resort

Some vacation options today are designed with dogs in mind. These doggie vacations take two forms: Dog resorts with planned activities, and dog resorts without.

Those places with planned activities are known as *dog camps.* The organizers rent a campground, school campus, or a similar location for part of the year and bring in trainers, lecturers, and other experts to teach campers and their human companions about various dog sports. It's not as serious as it sounds, though: Dog camps leave plenty of time for hiking, fetch, silly games, and just plain hanging out with other dogs.

The other kind of dog resort is dog-friendly to the maximum extent possible, with tile floors and easy-to-clean furnishings. You can do as you please at these types of resorts.

Try Ruffing It!

Some people spend their vacation in the great outdoors — and they want to take their dogs with them. Fortunately, sturdy, well-designed packs are on the market designed to let your dog carry his share of the load, and even some of yours. An adult dog in top condition can carry up to a quarter of his weight, evenly distributed in a properly fitting pack. Get your dog used to the feel of the pack on short walks and trips and gradually build up the weight and distance.

Dogs aren't welcome everywhere; the biggest danger to the future of canine backpacking is other hikers, more so than wild beasts. Don't give the dog haters any ammunition: Keep your dog under control, and that means on-leash in areas with other people or animals. Take something to bury waste, or supplies to pack it back out.

If Your Dog Can't Go with You

When you have to leave your best canine companion behind, you're better off checking out your options ahead of time. Ask your friends, neighbors, and co-workers what they do with their pets when they're gone. Ask your veterinarian, too, for referrals to pet sitters or kennels. Remember, the people you ask may have different criteria for selecting a service than you do.

When you have a service in mind, whether a kennel or sitter, call and ask for references, and then check them out. Ask about professional affiliations, such as the American Boarding Kennel Association or National Association of Pet Sitters.

No matter what kind of care you choose for your pet while you're gone, make your arrangements early. Pet sitters and boarding kennels are booked weeks and sometimes months in advance for peak travel times such as summer or the winter holidays.